Come, Let Us

Magnify the Lord

the

Come, Let Us Magnify the Lord

**Presenting a heart of gratitude and praise
to the God of all grace**

"O magnify the LORD
with me, and let us
exalt His name together"
(Psalm 34:3).

Eddie Cloer

R ESOURCE □
P UBLICATIONS
2205 S. Benton
Searcy, AR 72143

DEDICATION

To our daughter-in-law,
Lindsay (Snow) Cloer,
A lovely princess,
Charming, conscientious, caring,
Committed to following her Lord,
A dedicated Christian young woman,
Who, I believe, seeks to be truly
what God wants a woman to be,
And who is the Christian we cherish
as our daughter-in-law.

"Charm is deceitful and beauty is vain,
but a woman who fears the Lord,
she shall be praised"
(Proverbs 31:30).

"Thy gifts are strewn upon my way
Like sands upon the great seashore."
—F. W. Faber

CONTENTS

PREFACE

Join me in giving special praise and thanksgiving to God, not for a day, not for a month, but for a season of time. Here are forty-two thanksgiving meditations that will encourage you in voicing your love and appreciation to the God of heaven, the One to whom all thanksgiving goes.

I am suggesting that you gather your family and have a home devotional in which you give thanks to God. As Christians, we reside in Christ, where we have received all spiritual blessings in and through Him in heavenly places (Ephesians 1:3). The Spirit through Paul has told us who we are, what we have, and where we are going. As Christians, we should be the happiest and most grateful people on earth. Upon His people the culmination of God's eternal planning has descended and reached its fulfillment. We have received and now enjoy what the prophets only dimly saw and yearned to have.

The tragedy is that many people have been blessed

bountifully of God but they do not acknowledge those blessings. They never say "Thank You" to God. They never praise Him for what He has done. Let us open our eyes to who God is and what He has done for us and then freely acknowledge His manifold blessings upon our pilgrimage through this world.

Had it not been for the Lord's lovingkindness and guidance, think of where we would be! Join with me in praising Him for the wonderful bounties He has poured out upon us and upon those around us.

> *"But thanks be to God, who gives us the victory through our Lord Jesus Christ" (1 Corinthians 15:57).*

Eddie Cloer

1

PRAISE WITHOUT CEASING

"So we Your people and the sheep of Your pasture will give thanks to You forever; to all generations we will tell of Your praise" (Psalm 79:13).

"Through Him then, let us continually offer up a sacrifice of praise to God, that is, the fruit of lips that give thanks to His name" (Hebrews 13:15).

Praise, by definition, is giving thanks to God for what He has done. One wonderful message in these two verses is that continual praise is part of the life of the believer. We know what God has done for us in the past, and we are confident of what He will do for us tomorrow; therefore, we joyfully extol Him and give thanks to Him.

The "always" of spirituality is found three times in 1 Thessalonians 5: "Rejoice always"; "Pray without ceasing"; and "In everything give thanks" (1 Thessalonians 5:16–18a). Implied in these three injunctions is a fourth: "Praise Him without ceasing."

As we begin a season of praising our Father and His Son, Jesus, let us commit ourselves to three great praise resolutions.

The first resolution: "We will remember to praise Him." We will not receive His gifts and go on our way without expressing adoration and thanksgiving to Him. Whatever we may face, we will have one resolve firmly settled in our hearts: We will give thanks to Him. Praise is never out of place. Even when we are in a smog of confusion, we will praise Him for all that He has done.

The second resolution: "We will commit ourselves to praising Him continually." Our praise will not be spasmodic and once-in-a-while; it will be perennial, ever new, and continually flowing upward and outward. Don't let yourself talk to you; you talk to yourself. With a resolute commitment, say to your heart, "The praise of God will be the pattern of my life. It will be a constant attitude that I will seek to maintain."

The third resolution: "We will resolve to teach others to praise Him." We will pass this sweet spirit of praise on to the generations that will follow us. Our joyous praise of God will go up to Him and out to others, for we will teach our children and our neighbors to praise God. We have learned in our spiritual journey that one way to tell whether or not we have succeeded with our families is to ask ourselves, "Are our children praising God?" If they are, we have been a success; if they are not, we have failed. All other standards of measuring human achievement are faulty.

In times of great joy and in the crumbled ruins of disaster, we will praise the God of our salvation. In whatever situation we find ourselves, we will lift up our voices to Him in thanksgiving. Nothing, not even the greatest of all tragedies, will be allowed to interrupt our blessing His name and giving adoration to God our Father and Jesus His Son.

When we think of gratitude in the life of the Christian, two words come to mind: "praise" and "persistence." Christians are aware of how dependent on God they are, and they express their understanding of this undeniable fact in their daily and public thanksgiving to Him.

We cannot praise Him continuously,
but we can praise Him continually.
So, come, let us magnify the Lord together.

In prayer, give thanks to God
for the privilege of praising Him.

2

LIVING BEYOND OURSELVES

"Let the peoples praise You, O God; let all the peoples praise You"; "God blesses us, that all the ends of the earth may fear Him" (Psalm 67:5, 7).

"And pray on my behalf, that utterance may be given to me in the opening of my mouth, to make known with boldness the mystery of the gospel" (Ephesians 6:19).

The Christian lives in a new spiritual dimension: He walks on the level of the transformed mind (Romans 12:2). Thus God has asked that we write "Beyond this" over all that we receive and do.

Beyond . . . receiving His pardon, let us walk with God. Our Father does not want us to be satisfied with the forgiveness of sins. He wants us to go beyond our purging and enter into a life with Him to which pardon has opened the door. Godly sorrow means that we are sorry for our sins because they have destroyed our relationship with God. Forgiveness is the divine means of leaving the path of sin, a time of embracing the new freedom in which we walk with God.

Beyond . . . the provisions we have enjoyed, let us seek the blessings of others. God has blessed us so that we might be a blessing to others. He preserved the Israelite nation so that Israel might be a light to the nations. We have heard His commission, and we yearn to be spent in fulfilling it. Where He leads us, we will follow, though His footprints lead us through dens of iniquity to rescue the perishing.

Beyond . . . asking for what we need and want, let us engage in praising God for what He has done. Our prayers are mostly made up of lists of what we think we ought to have. Spiritual growth means that we have gone past our requests to rejoicing in who God is and what He has done through sending His Son. We move from petition to praise, from appeals for more to appreciation for what we already have.

Beyond . . . living for ourselves, let us live for and with others. God wants us to pray and praise with His heart, a heart that takes in all the people of the earth. Paul urged us, "Do nothing from selfishness or empty conceit, but with humility of mind regard one another as more important than yourselves" (Philippians 2:3).

The Pharisees and the Sadducees of Jesus' day settled for a religion, while God wanted them to experience a spiritual life. He wanted them to allow the Law to lead them to Christ, the true religion of the Christian Age. The Law was the means, not the end—an avenue, not an accomplishment. They stopped with the Law, while God wanted them to go on to the life that the Law was designed to bring. Let us make sure that we do not allow the things of God to become our stopping places; rather, we must let the things of God take us to the place of communion, fellowship, and life with God.

Someone has said, "One can see a person's character by noticing how often he says 'Thank you' during the day." Likewise, one can see the true character of a person's spirituality by observing how often he says "Thank You" to God.

In prayer, praise God for the ability that He has given you to go beyond yourself and live in the "beyond this" spiritual dimension.

3

THE JOY OF PRAISING HIM

"Sing for joy in the Lord, O you righteous ones; praise is becoming to the upright" (Psalm 33:1).

"But you are a chosen race, a royal priesthood, a holy nation, a people for God's own possession, so that you may proclaim the excellencies of Him who has called you out of darkness into His marvelous light" (1 Peter 2:9b).

The Christian should be adept at praising God. This high and holy activity should be normal with us. From the first verse of Psalm 33 and from 1 Peter 2:9, we see the nature of praising the Lord.

The praise of God is an expression of gratitude. Praise is an overflow and outflow of thanksgiving. We celebrate thanksgiving in America, but many families do not know whom to thank. The Christian does.

The praise of God should naturally emerge from

joy. The happiness God has given us should express itself in extolling Him. Worship is to be a joyous occasion, with worshipers gathering to sing with happy hearts filled with gratefulness.

The praise of God should be given by the people of God. Praise of God is a family trait. The desire to give thanks to God rises up daily in the hearts of His redeemed people. God is a righteous God, and He wants His righteous ones, the ones made righteous by His Son's blood, to worship Him (see Isaiah 6:4, 5).

The praise of God should be a recurring theme. We sing a new song each time we come together because we have new reasons to praise our God. In 1 John 2:7, John said that he was writing about the command to love one another, an old commandment that had become new. It was old in age but new in quality. Jesus had made it new because He had shown His disciples how to exhibit it. So it is with praise. God's recent mercy gives us a reason to add new songs of praise to our worship. We may sing an old song, but we sing it in a new way or with new meaning.

The Christian is motivated regularly to lift up his heart in praise to God. He is constrained by his joys, his redeemed life, the recurring mercies of God, the precious Word of God, and the gratitude of his heart for all that God has done. Let us eagerly respond to every impulse to praise our Father, pouring out before His throne the love for God that we have in our hearts.

"Who can speak of the mighty deeds of the Lord, or can show forth all His praise?" (Psalm 106:2).

One who has truly been saved by God's grace will find praising Him to be the easiest and the most natural thing to do.

In prayer, praise God for the redemption that you have in Christ.

4

DECLARING HIS GOODNESS

"And my tongue shall declare Your right-eousness and Your praise all day long" (Psalm 35:28).

"After these things I looked, and behold, a great multitude which no one could count, . . . and they cry out with a loud voice, saying, 'Salvation to our God who sits on the throne, and to the Lamb'" (Revelation 7:9, 10).

It is always appropriate to praise God. In times of happiness and in times of difficulty, we can offer to the Lord the adoration of our hearts.

Let us rejoice in who God is. Who can look at God and not break forth in praise? When one realizes who He is and what He is like, all of the troubles and trials of life fade away. When we get to heaven, we will be overcome by the wonder of His goodness.

Let us exult in His everlasting gospel. His salvation

is the great salvation of which the prophets spoke and which our Lord fulfilled. It is the heart of the Bible. If one cannot praise God for His gospel, he simply does not understand it or has not tasted of its sweetness. God's offer of salvation reflects His great love, and anyone who wishes may be saved by His grace. His mercy reaches out to all people. It will lift the vilest sinner all the way to heaven, and it is extended so continually that we have to utilize the word "long-suffering" even to describe it.

Let us rejoice in His strength. He holds the universe in the palm of His hand. He commands the seas, telling them their dimensions and limitations. He sustains the earth, providing for its continuity and energy. He watches over His own people, sustaining them in every situation. Nothing is too hard for Him. He has all power. No problem is too big or too little for Him to handle. He walks with His people through fire, keeping them safe; and when they emerge, they do not even have the smell of smoke upon them.

Let us rejoice in His daily compassions. Beneath His overarching love lie His continual compassions and kindnesses. We can say with Jeremiah that these daily mercies are "new every morning." We see them in the leaves, the air, the food we eat, the friends we have, and a multitude of blessings that we could not count if we were to dedicate days to the task. Each day is a day of God's gracious deeds. He sends the rain on the earth, covers His people with care, and fills the skies with His sunshine.

Every person on earth at all times and in all places has numerous reasons for praising God. It is never out of place to lift our hearts and voices to God in extolling His name.

Can our tongues and hearts be used
for any nobler purpose than praising God
for numerous mercies?

In prayer, praise God for His daily mercies.

5

HIS HAND HAS BEEN UPON US

> *"For You are my hope; O Lord God, You are my confidence from my youth. By You I have been sustained from my birth; You are He who took me from my mother's womb; my praise is continually of You"; "Do not cast me off in the time of old age; do not forsake me when my strength fails" (Psalm 71:5, 6, 9).*

God's gracious care is brought out in Psalm 71. Its overarching coverage thrills us beyond expression. Meditate upon it and marvel at God's goodness.

He watched over us with His kind providence before we were ever born. He not only brought us into this world, but He extended grace to us while we were in our mothers' wombs. He told Jeremiah that He had His eye on him before he ever made his entrance into this world (Jeremiah 1:5, 18). God was involved, in some way far beyond our ability to understand, in our conception, in our embryonic growth, and in our birth.

He has had us under His care all through the years, whether we have known it or not. We sought Him, but later we found out that we sought Him because He was seeking us.

> Thy mercy heard my infant prayer;
> Thy love with all a mother's care
>   Sustained my childish days:
> Thy goodness watched my ripening youth,
> And pressed my heart to love Thy truth,
>   And filled my lips with praise.
>
> —Robert Grant

He has made us a wonder to those around us. How could this be? Could God turn our pitiful lives into a wonder? Yes, He does it for all of His devoted followers. He takes weeds and turns them into flowers. He changed Rahab, a prostitute, into a paragon of virtue, making her a part of the Lord's lineage. He took a grasping tax collector, Matthew, and made him into a gospel writer. He took a son of thunder, John, and changed him into an apostle of love.

Not only is He with us now, but He is also in the future waiting for us to arrive. When we get there, we will find that God has gone ahead and prepared the way for us. He is "preparing us" for what He is "preparing for us." I do not have to worry about yesterday, today, or tomorrow.

He is now a habitable rock for our protection. The believer is a Rock dweller. He is near us as a great, impregnable fortress, and we must remember that we are dwelling in Him whenever storms arise. He is our ever-present help—accessible, invincible, and eternal.

One cannot praise God unless he thinks about who He is and what He has done. Thinking and remembering must come before praising. Let us think, remember, and praise Him!

*Praise to God is really nothing more than
making a list of what God has done
for you and then thanking Him
for His kindnesses.*

*In prayer, thank and praise God for
watching over you all through the years.*

6

"WHO MAY STAND BEFORE HIM?"

> *"Who may ascend into the hill of the Lord? And who may stand in His holy place? He who has clean hands and a pure heart, who has not lifted up his soul to falsehood and has not sworn deceitfully" (Psalm 24:3, 4).*

> *"But an hour is coming, and now is, when the true worshipers will worship the Father in spirit and truth; for such people the Father seeks to be His worshipers. God is spirit, and those who worship Him must worship in spirit and truth" (John 4:23, 24).*

The first part of the answer to the questions in Psalm 24:3, questions that are also implied in John 4:23, "Who may ascend into the hill of the Lord? And who may stand in His holy place?" is "Those who come in the robes of godliness." These two passages stress purity of heart and life, and the robes of godliness may be divided into three parts: outward, inward, and relational garments.

The outward requirement is that we come with clean hands. This expression is a poetic depiction of righteous actions. The hand stands for deeds. It is figurative because the hand cannot do anything without direction from the head. Our hands do not act; we act with our hands.

The inward requirement is that we come with pure hearts. This godly heart does not lift itself up to falsehood and does not fall down before the gods of men. God wants integrity above all things. An honest heart can be taught and will respond favorably to faithful teaching. A dishonest heart is dirty, and as such, cannot bring the kind of worship that God will accept.

The relationship requirement is that we come with faithful tongues. The true worshiper does not lie to others or swear falsely to others. His word is his bond. Those who know him need no other surety than his word. His words match up with the commitment of his heart.

The preacher must prepare for a sermon, and the worshipers must prepare for worship. The preparation by the worshipers is made by washing the hands of filthy deeds, cleansing the heart of evil, and removing deceit from the tongue.

We are to approach God with reverence and purity of life—reverence because He is our Creator and

Redeemer, and purity because of His holy nature.

The worship of Yahweh is the greatest single privilege that human beings ever know—and one of our supreme duties, from which no human being is excused. Proper worship requires that we come as cleansed people with the appropriate offerings, joyfully giving adoration to the Great King.

Worship is given to God; it should be based upon what God wants, not upon what we want.

In prayer, praise God because of who He is, His perfect attributes, and His amazing love.

7

NATURE'S SONG OF PRAISE

"The heavens are telling of the glory of God; and their expanse is declaring the work of His hands. Day to day pours forth speech, and night to night reveals knowledge" (Psalm 19:1, 2).

"Thus You prepare the earth. You water its furrows abundantly, You settle its ridges, You soften it with showers, You bless its growth. You have crowned the year with Your bounty, and Your paths drip with fatness" (Psalm 65:9d–11).

The goodness of God is strewn across the world of nature like a thick coat of paint across a canvas. He has manifested His love for mankind by the generous supplies He provides through the rain and a million other acts of kindness. Let us observe God's actions and give thanks for what He has done for us through the world of nature.

He sustains it. Nature could not continue without God's supportive hand. Jesus is pictured as "uphold[ing] all things by the word of His power" (Hebrews 1:3). Paul said of Him, "He is before all things, and in Him all things hold together" (Colossians 1:17). He not only created it, but He provides the divine energy that makes it work.

He shows His power through it. Being "girded with might" (Psalm 65:6), God established the mountains by His strength, the writer of this psalm says. How can anyone look at a violent storm, the Grand Canyon, the hills decked with grass, or the millions of stars that light up the darkened sky and not be left speechless in the presence of His power! Paul said that the creation of the world displays God's invisible attributes and divine power for all who have eyes to clearly see (Romans 1:20).

He displays His grace in it. One would be hard-pressed to find a more picturesque portrayal of God's goodness in nature than the latter part of this psalm. He waters the earth, making its pastures grow and giving moisture to its vegetation. He covers its fields with grain, walking through the fields as if pulling a wagon of good things and dropping off from His wagon His bounties of fruit, crops, and many other good things. Anyone who seriously looks around will see where God has been. A trail of precious gifts tell of His having come through.

Every day we are greeted with a testimony of God's goodness, an anthem of praise, by the world of God's creation around us. Let us add our voices of praise to the faithful, recurring, silent chorus of nature.

*No one can read God's Word
or God's World and not see
His goodness splashed upon every page.*

*In prayer, praise God for what He
has revealed to us about His character
from the world of nature.*

8

BEHOLDING GOD'S GLORY

"The voice of the Lord makes the deer to calve and strips the forests bare; and in His temple everything says, 'Glory!'" (Psalm 29:9).

"Seraphim stood above Him, each having six wings: with two he covered his face, and with two he covered his feet, and with two he flew. And one called out to another and said, 'Holy, Holy, Holy, is the Lord of hosts, the whole earth is full of His glory'" (Isaiah 6:2, 3).

God is all-glorious, whether we choose Him to be so or not. By our lives and our lips, by our accomplishments and achievements, we cannot add one glimmer of glory to His character. He is self-sufficient and transcendent in glory.

How, then, do we give glory to God?

We give glory to God when we observe who He is. We have not treated God right until we have studied

Him and recognized who He actually is. We meditate on the Scriptures and observe the world of nature around us—and we come to know God.

We give glory to Him by beholding His glory. We cannot tell of His glory until we see it. Sometimes we look but do not see, we study but do not understand. We may know the facts about God and not know God. We can absorb information about God without understanding His glory.

We give glory to Him when we proclaim His glory. We reflect it in our lives, we tell others about it with our lips, and we give God thanks for revealing it to us in all the ways that He does.

All the created creatures and things of the earth give glory to God naturally by doing what they were created to do. A star shines down on us and preaches God's glory. It has no voice with which to speak, so it makes known His splendor by what it does. Of all God's creation, we are the only living creatures who have to discipline themselves to give glory to God. We have to study God, behold His grandeur, then proclaim the glory we have seen.

Someone has said, "When I get to heaven, I have about five questions I want to ask God!" Responding to such a remark, someone else has said, "When you get there, you will be so overwhelmed by what you see that you will forget your questions, and all you will be able to do is praise Him."

33

Indeed, when we stand before His throne, perhaps we will be so immersed in His greatness that all we can do is utter, "Glory! Glory! Glory!" If the angelic beings looked at a raging wind, the storm of God, and cried, "Glory!" will we be able to do more when we see the God of the storm? We are not ready for heaven until we are recognizing and declaring the great glory of God the Father and His Son, Jesus Christ.

When we walk with the glorious God,
His glory shines upon us and through us—
even out to the beholding world.

In prayer, praise God for His wondrous glory,
as you resolve anew to proclaim it to others.

9

PERENNIAL GRATITUDE

"Sing praise to the Lord, you His godly ones, and give thanks to His holy name" (Psalm 30:4).

"And yet He did not leave Himself without witness, in that He did good and gave you rains from heaven and fruitful seasons, satisfying your hearts with food and gladness" (Acts 14:17).

How can one serve God? We cannot bring Him food, for He is never hungry. We cannot give Him money, since He already owns it all. We cannot fight battles for Him, for He can speak a word and wipe away the strongest enemy.

Nevertheless, we see throughout the Scriptures one obvious gift that we can give Him: We can express gratitude for His numerous gifts.

We can respond to His great acts of mercy with thankful hearts. The writer of Psalm 30 did. He saw that God had extended his life, and he quickly voiced the appreciation that a child of God should have. He gave God the thanksgiving of his soul.

We can exhort other believers to give thanks to Him. The psalmist urged the godly ones around him to praise God. All those who have been blessed by God (and this would include the whole world of people) have the obligation of giving thanks to God. We can encourage the people around us to join us in praising God.

We can have a permanent attitude of gratitude that shows up in our daily walk with Him. The psalmist did. Thanksgiving is not a day, but a continual attitude. The Christian takes seriously Paul's injunction regarding continual gratitude: "In everything give thanks" (1 Thessalonians 5:18a).

One man prayed, "Lord, You have given us so many blessings. We ask for only one more gift: Give us grateful hearts."

The person who does not have a grateful heart
toward his or her true Benefactor, God,
is no better than the brute beasts of the field.

In prayer, give thanks for the blessings
that encircle you, such as your family,
your health, and a thousand other bounties.

10

GOD'S STRONG ARM

"The cords of death encompassed me, and the torrents of ungodliness terrified me. The cords of Sheol surrounded me; the snares of death confronted me. In my distress I called upon the Lord, and cried to my God for help; He heard my voice out of His temple, and my cry for help before Him came into His ears" (Psalm 18:4–6).

"Yet for this reason I found mercy, so that in me as the foremost, Jesus Christ might demonstrate His perfect patience as an example for those who would believe in Him for eternal life" (1 Timothy 1:16).

In Psalm 18 David spoke of having been brought out of a great tragedy that he likened to death. All of us have faced grave circumstances—physical illnesses, automobile accidents, or other tragedies. What should be our reaction to God's preservation?

Let us give God the credit for our salvation. David realized that God was the one who brought deliverance, although he might have had a small hand in the victory. God often uses us in His work. However, David was wise enough to recognize that God was really the great Deliverer.

Let us praise Him for what He has done. One of the basic responses we can make to God's goodness is to praise Him for His grace and to share the blessings of His goodness with others. Both David and Paul wrote of how God had delivered them so that others could see His mercy and rejoice with them.

Let us plant in our minds the great truth that God is good. Since we have seen God's grace, let us resolve that we will never forget it. He has answered us according to His love. God always covers people with His love before He brings judgment upon them because of their impenitence.

Let us remember to praise God in the assembly. When we gather with the saints for worship, let us praise God out of our appreciation for what He has done for us. Someone has said, "God should not be praised alone." All have been blessed by Him, and all should give thanks to Him.

We should provoke one another to love and good deeds (Hebrews 10:24), but we should also provoke one another to the praise of the Lord. We can do this exhorting by example as well as by word. What will it do to others when they see us praising God out of joyful hearts that are full of gratitude for His kindnesses? Surely, they will take note and will be encouraged to have the same attitude of praise.

David had been through a trying experience, but he had come out on the other side more conscious of God's goodness, protection, and strength. He had gained a greater appreciation of how gracious God had been to him.

God, at times, allows us to experience trouble so that we may see more clearly His strong arm, our failures, and His infinite grace.

Give thanks to God for delivering you—
for the times you know about and
for the times that are hidden behind
the veil of His providence.

In prayer, praise God for the times He has
delivered you. You may want to name
some of them specifically and then thank
Him for all of them in general.

11

THE GOD OF ABUNDANCE

> *"O Lord, in Your strength the king will be glad, and in Your salvation how greatly he will rejoice! You have given him his heart's desire, and You have not withheld the request of his lips" (Psalm 21:1, 2).*

> *"Now to Him who is able to do far more abundantly beyond all that we ask or think . . ." (Ephesians 3:20).*

How does God answer His children's prayers? As we consider this question, two words come to mind: "abundantly" and "generously."

Let us rejoice that God is a prayer answering God. In Psalm 21, the king and the people petitioned God, and He heard their desires. We can say something similar: Christians pray, and God hears us. On the basis of Psalm 21:1, 2 and Ephesians 3:20, we can confidently affirm that God answers the prayers of His people. Are we not glad?

He gives us more than we ask. The king asked for life, and God gave him a long life. The people asked for victory, and God gave it. Similarly, Christians pray and He gives us more than we can ask or think.

He fills our hearts with gladness. God did not reluctantly answer their prayers; He did it with the enjoyment of a father responding to the requests of his son. His generosity in response to our prayers has filled our hearts with the joy of grateful love.

He condescends to dwell with us. He not only gives us His provisions, but also, and more importantly, gives us His presence. We find His fellowship to be greater than all His gifts. Walking with the Giver is far more wonderful than partaking of His gifts.

When God answers our prayers, our rejoicing quickly turns to praise, for we have seen how graciously, lavishly, and lovingly He has assisted us.

It is easy for us to give thanks to God for His sending us Jesus; but right now, let us give thanks for the fact that Jesus gave us God. Read John 14:6.

In prayer, praise God for sending Jesus who brought us His supreme gift to mankind: God.

12

WHERE GOD STANDS

"Because Your lovingkindness is better than life, my lips will praise You. So I will bless You as long as I live"; "For You have been my help, and in the shadow of Your wings I sing for joy. My soul clings to You; Your right hand upholds me" (Psalm 63:3, 4a, 7, 8).

"Nevertheless, the firm foundation of God stands, having this seal, 'The Lord knows those who are His' . . ." (2 Timothy 2:19).

Should we not ask, "Where does God stand?" He is the one supreme fact of life. He created us, sustains us, and is the destiny toward which all of us are moving. Is it not essential that we discover how He thinks, what His aspirations are, and what He seeks to accomplish in us?

God's revelation to us gives foundational truths about where He stands that fill us with amazement, assurance, and anticipation.

God stands on the side of His servants. Voltaire, an atheist, said, "God is on the side of the biggest battalions." He was wrong. God is on the side of His faithful people.

Psalm 63 may have in its background Absalom's attempt to take over the kingdom from his father, David (2 Samuel 17; 18). Absalom had mustered an army, but his large force was only strong in human terms. He was going against David with the strength of physical might alone. While Absalom may have had the bigger battalions, David had something Absalom did not have: He had God. Guess who won.

David was a righteous man who loved God and was seeking to serve Him. God stood with His righteous servant. He always does.

God stands with His promises. David had God's pledge that the throne was his. To drive David permanently off that throne, Absalom would first have to defeat God, the God who had chosen David.

Never ask God to violate His word. If you do, you are asking God to do something that He cannot do. He cannot lie (Titus 1:2). One truth that we can always count on is that God will always tell the truth. We can rest assured that He will be faithful to every promise He has made.

God stands in communion and fellowship with His servants. Like any parent, God wants to be with His children. The joys of David's relationship with God cannot be fully described. He exclaimed in prayer, "Because Your lovingkindness is better than life, my lips will praise You"; "My soul is satisfied as with marrow and fatness, and my mouth offers praises with joyful lips" (Psalm 63:3, 5). David walked with God daily, but he was not satisfied with his current relationship with God. Though He knew God, he cried, "My soul thirsts for You, my flesh yearns for You, in a dry and weary land where there is no water" (Psalm 63:1b). David always yearned to go deeper and deeper into that relationship.

God stands with those who trust Him. Robust faith in the fulfillment of God's plans sustained David during his dark night of trial. When difficulties came, he would not quickly conclude that God had been defeated. He believed that, in time, he would see the victory of the Lord. His heart was braced by the truth that God would always come to the aid of the person who had put his faith in Him.

When we know where God stands, we also know where we should stand. He stands with His faithful servants, with His promises, in communion and fellowship with His servants, and with those who trust in Him. Therefore, we know how we should live. We will put our faith in Him and never waver in our commitment. As we walk in faith, we are confident that He will walk with us. His presence with us means everything. With Paul we can say, "What then shall we say to these things? If God is for us, who is against us?" (Romans 8:31).

The question is not "Is God standing with me?" The question is "Am I standing with God?"

In prayer, praise God for His righteousness which guarantees to us where God will always stand.

13

THE GOD WHO GOES BEFORE

". . . 'Arise! For this is the day in which the Lord has given Sisera into your hands; behold, the Lord has gone out before you'" (Judges 4:14a).

"For You are my rock and my fortress; for Your name's sake You will lead me and guide me" (Psalm 31:3).

"For I believe God that it will turn out exactly as I have been told" (Acts 27:25b).

God has always been the God who has gone before us. Think of the flower girls who go before the bride, throwing out flowers to decorate her path. God has been to us like those little princesses decorating the pathway of the bride with beautiful things, but in a far greater sense. He has gone before us tossing out His grace, precious gifts, and numerous other favors.

He has gone before us in this life. When we came

into this world, we found that God had already been here and had prepared everything for us. He had good parents waiting on us; and if He did not, He had prepared other ways of caring for us. He had a world waiting to sustain us, people who would love us, and opportunities that would invite us to grow.

He has gone before us in the spiritual realm. He has been planning for us through three biblical ages. He brought Christ into the world, He created the church for us, and He had the everlasting gospel waiting for us to be our means of salvation. All spiritual blessings were available for us when we made the decision to put on Jesus in baptism (Galatians 3:27; Ephesians 1:3).

On the basis of what He has done in the past, we can trust that He has gone before us in eternity. Jesus said, "I go to prepare a place for you" (John 14:3a). When we step over to life's other side, we will find that God is waiting for us with far greater blessings than we have seen in this life. Paul said that to depart and be with Christ is far better than to remain here (Philippians 1:23).

God went before Israel to fight the battles and give them victories, and we have found Him to be the God who goes before us as well. He has smoothed out a road for us and made the journey a delight.

As we make our way through the wilderness of this world, it helps us to remember that God has preceded us, removing the tangled vines and the wild beasts of the future. Let us follow His leadership, and all will be well—in life, in the church, and in eternity.

Because of His eternal plenitudes,
God cannot be confined to time.
From eternity past, through time,
and into eternity future, He guides our way.

In prayer, praise God for His going
before you, making the lavish preparations
for your salvation, your spiritual joy,
and your life with Him.

14

GOD, THE ONLY CHAMPION

"Be exalted, O Lord, in Your strength; we will sing and praise Your power" (Psalm 21:13).

"But in all these things we overwhelmingly conquer through Him who loved us" (Romans 8:37).

When we return from the field of a spiritual battle, savoring a decisive victory, we are prone to congratulate ourselves. We may even say, with a degree of puffed-up pride, "You did a great job!" This psalm was written to remind the king and his people that God is the only Champion, the only Victor. In addition, in a New Testament parallel, Romans 8 announces the great victories the Christian has through Christ. The words of the psalm guided the king and the people into proper thinking about what had occurred. Romans 8 will likewise assist us in having the right attitude toward the spiritual successes we enjoy.

In one of the parables that Jesus told, a rich man is pictured as reasoning "to himself" (Luke 12:17). What this man said to himself brought about his downfall. He listened to the wrong preacher; he took to heart a frail and faulty message.

Let us ask ourselves, "What are we saying to ourselves about God?" Psalm 21 and Romans 8 remind us to speak faithfully about God in our hearts.

What we say to ourselves is the true measure of our spirituality. If someone could look into my heart and observe what I am saying to myself about God and spiritual concerns, my true spiritual qualities would become known. I can mislead others with my actions, but my thoughts will present the true picture of what I am.

What we say to ourselves is the mainspring of life. Our thoughts constitute the source, the origin, of all our words and actions. The conversations that we carry on with ourselves form the fountainhead of the living that we do. No person rises above the thinking that he does deep within his soul. As someone has said, "We are not what we think we are; but what we think, we are."

What we say to ourselves is that part of us that is of greatest interest to God. It seems that God weighs our intent more than He does our actions (1 Samuel 16:7; 2 Corinthians 8:12). One young lady said to me, "God does not see our faces; He sees our hearts." She meant that God does not pay a lot of attention to what our faces look like but carefully watches our hearts. He wants to know what is going on in our innermost beings. First and foremost, we worship and serve God with our minds, by our private thoughts and aspirations about Him.

The Scriptures can help us. They reach within us and refine even the thoughts and intents of the heart (Hebrews 4:12). Let us allow the Scriptures to teach us how to think about God. Sometimes we read a verse and exclaim, "That's exactly what I was thinking!" Sometimes we read a passage and moan, "That's exactly what I should have been thinking!" For example, these two verses, Psalm 21:13 and Romans 8:37, help us to have the right view, the "praise God" view, of our triumphs over the devil.

*Let us think righteously, for in so doing
we are building a righteous life.*

*In prayer, praise God for the amazing
victories He has given you and the Scriptures
that help you to think correctly about them.*

15

Forgiveness, Complete and Eternal

"How blessed is he whose transgression is forgiven, whose sin is covered!" (Psalm 32:1).

"In Him we have redemption through His blood, the forgiveness of our trespasses, according to the riches of His grace which He lavished on us" (Ephesians 1:7, 8a).

Forgiveness is granted by Christ's blood through faith, repentance, confession of Jesus, and baptism into Christ (Acts 2:38–47). This truth points us to God's grace that is revealed in His pardoning of sins. What does forgiveness tell us about God?

He is able to pardon us. He did what was necessary to pardon us. Salvation would mean sending His Son to the cross to pay the price for our sins, so He did it. He is righteous and full of love. When we come to Him in faith, penitence, and obedience, He—through His divine plan—lovingly removes our transgressions and makes us His children.

He is willing to pardon us. The motivation behind God's forgiveness is His willingness to forgive us. It would be the greatest of all tragedies if God were able to forgive us but unwilling to do so. He does not wait for the sinner to come to Him; but, as is illustrated in the case of Adam (Genesis 3:9), He goes to the sinner and makes known His desire to welcome him back. Yes, "God, being rich in mercy . . . even when we were dead in our transgressions, made us alive together with Christ . . ." (Ephesians 2:4, 5).

He will guide after He has pardoned us. He does not stop with forgiveness. After we receive pardon, we receive the daily precepts; after the cleansing come Christian-life commands. Paul said that we have been redeemed "so that in the ages to come He might show the surpassing riches of His grace in kindness toward us in Christ Jesus" (Ephesians 2:7).

He does not just pardon us so that we may be forgiven; He pardons us so that we may live with Him. He saves us so that we may enjoy His fellowship in righteous living. After David told of his forgiveness and peace, God spoke and told him how He would guide, counsel, and teach him (Psalm 32:8). Even so in the Christian life, we see the wonders of His grace. Paul exclaimed, "For if while we were enemies we were reconciled to God through the death of His Son, much more, having been reconciled, we shall be saved by His life" (Romans 5:10).

Those who have come to know God's forgiveness find it easy to praise Him. We do it in word and song. Our conversations just dovetail into talking of what God has done. Most of our spiritual songs lift up His holy name because of the great salvation He has given. The great grace of the gospel displays the great heart of God! Let us praise the God of all grace for the salvation He has given and the life we have in Christ!

God does not forgive us just so we might be
free from sin and have eternal life;
He forgives us so that we might live and walk
with Him in fellowship and communion.

In prayer, praise God and His Son Jesus for
the forgiveness you have received through
obeying His gospel and walking in the light.

16

THE ROOTS OF JOY

"Be glad in the Lord and rejoice, you right-eous ones; and shout for joy, all you who are upright in heart" (Psalm 32:11).

"Rejoice always" (1 Thessalonians 5:16).

What is the source of our joy? From what does it spring?

Joy springs from walking with God. In His presence are joys forevermore (Psalm 16:11). As we walk with Him, the sunlight of His love surrounds us. His presence brings peace and an awareness of His provisions and protection. With these blessings comes a "joy inexpressible and full of glory." Peter wrote, "And though you have not seen Him, you love Him, and though you do not see Him now, but believe in Him, you greatly rejoice with joy inexpressible and full of glory" (1 Peter 1:8).

Joy springs from a righteous life. Sin steals our

joy; righteous living restores it. When we know that our sins are forgiven and we are walking in His counsel, we have a refreshment that comes from God Himself.

Joy springs from acknowledging the blessings of God. David had descended into the depths of misery and despair because of his sin. However, when he received the gifts of forgiveness and peace, he could rejoice once again. Earlier he had prayed, "Make me to hear joy and gladness"; "Restore to me the joy of Your salvation" (Psalm 51:8a, 12a). Through God's grace and David's repentance, his prayer was answered.

Joy is not something we grasp as if we were pursuing an ambition. It is a consequence of holiness, a result that arises from a happy life in God. We receive joy as the fruit of living in God's will. Sin is the joy robber; God is the joy giver.

Jesus came to make us holy, not happy;
but there is a joy that comes from
true holiness that towers above
the happiness of this world.

In prayer, praise God for the joy
He has given you through His goodness
and for your daily life in Him.

17

CONTEMPLATING GOD'S CARE

> *"Walk about Zion and go around her; count her towers; consider her ramparts; go through her palaces, that you may tell it to the next generation. For such is God, our God forever and ever; He will guide us until death"* (Psalm 48:12–14).

> *"And my God will supply all your needs according to His riches in glory in Christ Jesus. Now to our God and Father be the glory forever and ever. Amen"* (Philippians 4:19, 20).

The last part of Psalm 48 (vv. 12–14) portrays God's people meditating on God's protection and oversight of their nation at the temple. Philippians 4:19, 20 pictures Paul rejoicing in God's endless supply of resources for the Christian. What a wholesome and uplifting exercise it is to contemplate who God is and what He has done for His people!

His lovingkindness came into view. How kind and gracious God had been to them! He had always responded to their pleas and prayers with loving generosity and mercy. The dominate attribute in His actions was His grace.

His righteousness became evident. The people of God had found that His right hand was full of righteousness. In His dealings with them, He had always acted in character. Their experience with God confirmed that the foundation of His character is truth and the core of His character is love.

That His judgments were just and right became clear. All the decisions He had made were correct and appropriate. The villages throughout Judah were able to rejoice in the judgments of the Lord. Years later, Paul also declared that he had found God to be faithful and true to His Word.

It was obvious that He had blessed His people. He had dealt with them by His hand of bounty, making them into His nation. They had become what they were by His kind intention, and they were currently living through His provisions. The Israelites lived "from hand to mouth," from God's hand to their mouths.

He had directed them in the past, and His Word had been their means of success. He had shielded them from all harm. The reader of this psalm is urged to go look at Jerusalem and see how God had blessed it. The exhortation is "Go look at all the parts of Jerusalem.

Count her towers. Consider her ramparts. Go through her palaces. See how everything is in place. No part of the city has become marred by the enemy." After this contemplation, a resolve emerges to praise God for the rest of their lives. When one looks at the history of Jerusalem, he sees the grace of God and can only break forth in praise.

In 1999 I went with a tour group to Jerusalem. As we approached this eternal city, Don Shackelford informed us that when a Christian sees Jerusalem for the first time, he weeps. It is a moving experience for the believer to see this city because of God's association with it. When we looked at this historic city, we remembered God's faithful dealings with His people.

Paul urged the church at Philippi to remember that God had not failed in meeting their needs. He said that God had filled them with the fruit of righteousness through Jesus Christ, giving them a growth that had resulted unto the glory and praise of God (Philippians 1:11). He wanted these Philippian Christians to anticipate the same complete and all-sufficient grace in the future.

As we meditate on the character of the Lord, we see what they saw. We see His lovingkindness toward us, His righteousness, His faithful judgments, His supplying of our needs, and His guidance. Looking at the past brings us back to praising God, for in retrospect we see His kindness on every hand. God has met our needs

59

through the abundant riches we now have in Christ Jesus!

Every Christian has a history with God.
Look back over the way you have come,
and rejoice in what God has done for you.

In prayer, praise God for the wonderful
history that you have with Him.
Praise Him for His faithfulness,
truthfulness, and righteousness.

18

THE SOVEREIGN GOD

> *"Yours, O Lord, is the greatness and the power and the glory and the victory and the majesty, indeed everything that is in the heavens and the earth; Yours is the dominion, O Lord, and You exalt Yourself as head over all"* *(1 Chronicles 29:11).*

> *"And He made from one man every nation of mankind to live on all the face of the earth, having determined their appointed times and the boundaries of their habitation" (Acts 17:26).*

In verse 11 of this beautiful prayer of David in 1 Chronicles 29 and also in Paul's speech in Acts 17, we see the sovereignty of our God. He is not only our life, but He is also the Lord over us. His decisions are final, and His actions are uncontestable.

He lifts up. He raises up nations in accordance with His will. He controls not only individuals but also races of people. In His great providence He increases the power of some men and decreases the power of others.

He puts down. He destroys and eliminates as He sees fit. He brought down the great Roman Empire in His own way and at the time He chose. He changed the trade routes and destroyed Edom, who thought by living high in the rocky cliffs they were invincible (see Obadiah 3). He overcame Egypt through rearing the boy Moses in Pharaoh's palace (Exodus 2:10).

His plans are eternal. According to His righteous nature, He keeps His mighty actions within the confines of His eternal purposes. Our plans are fleeting, but God's plans stretch from eternity past to eternity future. Nothing that man does can ultimately destroy God's eternal will.

His people endure forever. Those who put their faith in Him become His people, and they will be blessed eternally. God takes those who have chosen Him and makes them into His nation. His promises undergird them, and His almighty hand shields them.

Every believer can exclaim with Paul, "Oh, the depth of the riches both of the wisdom and knowledge of God! How unsearchable are His judgments and unfathomable His ways! For who has known the mind of the Lord, or who became His counselor? Or who has first given to Him that it might be paid back to him again? For from Him and through Him and to Him are all things. To Him be the glory forever. Amen" (Romans 11:33–36).

Nothing should be more encouraging than thinking upon the sovereignty of God. He has no rival in time or eternity. There is no other God beside Him. No one can comprehend His might or absorb His wisdom. The safest place anyone can ever be is within the shadow of His wing.

The safest place for anyone to be is in the fellowship of God, surrounded by His love and His almighty, everlasting strength.

In prayer, praise God for making justly and righteously the decisions that only He can make.

19

HIS SAVING AND SUSTAINING GRACE

"Let Your lovingkindness, O Lord, be upon us, according as we have hoped in You" (Psalm 33:22).

"For the grace of God has appeared, bringing salvation to all men, instructing us to deny ungodliness and worldly desires and to live sensibly, righteously and godly in the present age" (Titus 2:11, 12).

Psalm 33 is a hymn of praise, and Titus 2:11, 12 is a declaration of who Jesus is. In both texts a special picture of God's grace is given. His lovingkindness is conveyed to us from five different viewpoints.

We see His grace in His Word. In verses 4 through 9 of the psalm, the Word of the Lord is described. His commands are filled with creative power and bring order out of chaos. "By the word of the Lord the heavens were made, and by the breath of His mouth all their host" (v. 6). "The earth is full of the lovingkindness of the Lord" (v. 5b). His Word has created this world for our living and enjoyment. "He gathers the waters of the sea together as a heap; He lays up the deeps in storehouses" (v. 7). Furthermore, with His Word, He has brought into existence His great scheme of redemption for our spiritual welfare.

We see His grace in His plan. His gracious plan is depicted in verses 10 and 11: "The Lord nullifies the counsel of the nations; He frustrates the plans of the peoples. The counsel of the Lord stands forever, the plans of His heart from generation to generation." He will not allow any disobedient nation to destroy His purposes. His counsel stands forever. He overrules the actions of mankind to accomplish His eternal designs.

We see His grace in His watch-care. In verses 13 through 19, a description of the Lord's watchfulness is given: "The Lord looks from heaven; He sees all the sons of men." He watches over the sons of men and never misses a move that they make. He observes His people so that He may guide them. "Behold, the eye of the Lord is on those who fear Him, on those who hope for His lovingkindness, to deliver their soul from death and to keep them alive in famine" (vv. 18, 19). He will not allow their needs to escape His notice.

We see His grace in His might. In verses 16 through

19, the Lord's great power is extolled: "The king is not saved by a mighty army; a warrior is not delivered by great strength." He uses His might in behalf of those who trust in Him. He delivers them from death, famine, and the other dragons of this world.

We see His grace in its fullness and completeness in the coming of Jesus. Titus 2:11, 12 says that the grace of God has appeared in the earthly advent of His Son. This appearance has brought salvation to all people. He became the sin offering for all who come to Him in obedient faith.

Grace flows from every part of God for those who put their faith in Him. His Word describes it; His plan provides it; His watch-care manifests it; His strength implements it; and His Son bought it at Calvary and brought it to us in the gospel. His grace brought us into His salvation, and His grace sustains us in His salvation as we walk with Him.

God's people are saved by grace because
they have entered it by the gospel and
continually stand in it by walking in the light.
They are saved by grace (the means)
through obedient faith (the method).

In prayer, praise God for the plenitude
of His amazing grace.

20

IN THE CIRCLE OF DIVINE FAVOR

"In peace I will both lie down and sleep, for You alone, O Lord, make me to dwell in safety" (Psalm 4:8).

"The steadfast of mind You will keep in perfect peace, because he trusts in You" (Isaiah 26:3).

Those who trust in God enjoy pure and supreme divine blessings. Through Psalm 4 and Isaiah 26, let us list a few of them and rejoice in them.

First, there is *deliverance in the time of trouble.* The psalmist said, "You have relieved me in my distress" (Psalm 4:1b). Throughout this psalm, mention is made of this wonderful truth. God is more than an emergency bellhop who runs to our aid every time we overextend ourselves. He is our Father who loves us, provides for us, protects us, and guides us.

There is *confidence that one's prayer will be heard.*

God listens sympathetically to His children. Each of us can say, "But know that the Lord has set apart the godly man for Himself; the Lord hears when I call to Him" (v. 3). Peter said, "For the eyes of the Lord are toward the righteous, and His ears attend to their prayer" (1 Peter 3:12a). God enjoys our fellowship as any earthly father would enjoy being with his children.

There is *the gracious favor of God*. The way to His grace is through His commands. The writer said, "Offer the sacrifices of righteousness, and trust in the Lord" (Psalm 4:5). God placed His obedient servant Noah in His ark of safety. God answers His people according to His lovingkindness and not according to their sins. One certainty of life is that God will be gracious to us when we come to Him in His appointed way.

There is *joy unspeakable that money cannot buy*. The writer said, "You have put gladness in my heart, more than when their grain and new wine abound" (v. 7). The gladness that God gives transcends all earthly honors and pleasures.

There is *peace in the midst of trial*. Surrounded by turmoil, the believer rests in the comfort and calmness of God's care (Isaiah 26:4). With enemies around him, the psalmist could say, "In peace I will both lie down and sleep" (Psalm 4:8a). God does not always deliver His servants from the fiery furnace; but, if they must walk in it, He ensures them that they will be protected.

68

There is *ultimate security*. "For You alone, O Lord, make me to dwell in safety" (v. 8b). The faithful followers of the Lord can rest with the confident hope that God is watching over them. They can sleep because God does not slumber! They are happy and secure in the hollow of His hand.

How attractive the righteous life is! We must not let enemies rob us of this life. The choice is ours, not theirs. Having prayed in truth and righteousness for those who had hurt him, the writer of the psalm could lie down to sleep in the peace and tranquillity that the Lord gives to the righteous heart.

The only refuge from God is a refuge in God.
He will either be a compassionate Father
or a consuming fire to us.

In prayer, praise God for the major blessings
He has provided for those who are
within the circle of His favor.

21

HIS COMPASSIONS RAN TO MEET US

"*Do not remember the iniquities of our fore-fathers against us; let Your compassion come quickly to meet us, for we are brought very low*" (*Psalm 79:8*).

"*But while he was still a long way off, his father saw him and felt compassion for him, and ran and embraced him and kissed him*" (*Luke 15:20b*).

The psalmist prayed, "Let Your compassion come quickly to meet us, for we are brought very low" (Psalm 79:8b). He believed that Israel was standing in need of God's grace and that she needed it quickly. He wanted His compassions to run to meet them. Think about this arresting expression.

He was saying, "Let Your compassion run to us

with Your forgiveness." Israel sought forgiveness because their sins had brought destruction upon them. He said, "Do not remember the iniquities of our fore-fathers against us. . . . And deliver us and forgive our sins for Your name's sake" (vv. 8, 9). Healing could not take place until they had received God's forgiveness.

He was saying, "Let Your compassion run to us and restore us." They wanted their entire spiritual life, their walk with God, their relationship with Him, restored. Incomplete, they sought wholeness; empty, they sought fullness. Israel was afraid the pagan nations would say of them, "Where is their God?" Looking upon the rubble of their city, they were afraid that they might say, "Their God is weak and impotent. He could not protect them from this disaster."

He was saying, "Let Your compassion run to us and claim us as Your own once again." Having been cast off as His people, Israel wanted to be God's faithful people once again, walking in the light of His presence, enjoying the approval of His face, rejoicing in His leadership and Lordship. He cried in prayer, "Help us, O God of our salvation, for the glory of Your name" (v. 9a). They had lost their identity as God's people, and they wanted that uniqueness back.

How wonderful it is to know that God runs with compassion to us! He does not walk; He runs. Listen anew to those beautiful words of Luke 15: "But while

71

he was still a long way off, his father saw him and felt compassion for him, and ran and embraced him and kissed him" (v. 20). The prodigal was coming home with only one plea on his heart: "May my father let his compassion come quickly to meet me!"

Saul, the great persecutor of God's people, asked Ananias to baptize him. We are not told what he said when he asked for baptism, but he could have said, "Baptize me, Ananias, because I want God's compassion to run quickly to me and cover all my sin."

This glorious truth we must always remember: When we were going down the aisle to become His child, God, in the crimson robes of compassion, ran to meet us. Let us praise God that He has run with His great compassion to us, granting us forgiveness, restoration, and sonship. He has been to us the God of all grace.

Let us remember that God's grace and truth go together. His truth opens the door to His grace. John said, "Grace and truth were realized through Jesus Christ" (John 1:17b).

In prayer, praise Him for His wonderful truth, which, upon our obedience to it, sends His grace running to meet us.

22

HIS GREAT SALVATION

"And my soul shall rejoice in the Lord; it shall exult in His salvation" (Psalm 35:9).

"Your lovingkindness, O Lord, extends to the heavens, your faithfulness reaches to the skies" (Psalm 36:5).

"May [you] be able to comprehend with all the saints what is the breadth and length and height and depth, and to know the love of Christ which surpasses knowledge" (Ephesians 3:18, 19a).

Some of the most beautiful expressions concerning God's lovingkindness and faithfulness are found in Psalm 36 and Ephesians 3. His lovingkindness "extends to the heavens"; His faithfulness "reaches to the skies" (Psalm 36:5). These expressions cause us to recognize the incomprehensible nature of God's offer of salvation to us.

His salvation is too good to miss. How can anyone ignore who God is and what He has done? Just think: The God who has created all things has extended His tender mercies and lovingkindness to frail, sinful people like us. The angels themselves view with breathless wonder what God has done for His sinful creation (1 Peter 1:12). One of the most remarkable truths in the Bible is that God loves us.

His salvation is too great to grasp. In our receiving of God's salvation, in our living of it, and in our lifetime of study of it, we will never be able to fully absorb its meaning (Ephesians 3:18, 19). Perhaps in eternity our greatest occupation will be that of comprehending His wonderful salvation more and more with purified minds.

His salvation is too grand to fail. Those who enter this covenant relationship with God have entered into God's eternal purpose. His salvation is greater in its design and creation than the creation of the universe itself. Angels look with amazement over it, the prophets sought to understand it more perfectly, and people of all the ages have been amazed at it.

Too great to grasp, too good to miss, too grand to fail! This description is true of salvation because it is true of God. He is too great to grasp. Who can comprehend God? He is too good to miss. Who can envision greater love and grace? He is too grand to fail us. His faithfulness and truth abide forever. In deep love and gratefulness, let us say with a writer of one of the psalms, "Blessed be the name of the Lord from this time forth and forever. From the rising of the sun to its setting the name of the Lord is to be praised" (Psalm 113:2, 3).

It has been said that when God makes a man, He breaks the mold. You are the only "you" God will ever make. Through His grace you are His by means of creation and by means of re-creation.

In prayer, praise God because you are His prized possession, a twice-born child of His.

23

UNDER THE WINGS OF HIS LOVE

"And the children of men take refuge in the shadow of Your wings. They drink their fill of the abundance of Your house; and You give them to drink of the river of Your delights. For with You is the fountain of life; in Your light we see light" (Psalm 36:7b–9).

"Blessed be the God and Father of our Lord Jesus Christ, who according to His great mercy has caused us to be born again to a living hope through the resurrection of Jesus Christ from the dead" (1 Peter 1:3).

Five images are used in Psalm 36 and 1 Peter 1 to convey the bounties God gives to those who love Him.

First, God is described as our life-giver (1 Peter 1:3). He brought about our new birth through the gospel of His Son. With His great mercy, He has bestowed upon us a new life, and with it, a new hope.

Second, God is pictured as a host in His house,

providing for His guests an abundant feast in addition to their fellowship with Him (Psalm 36:8a). His guests are completely satisfied. His goodness and provisions are ever available to those who live with Him.

Third, God is seen as a keeper of a garden in which those who come to Him are given unlimited access to a river that flows with endless pleasures (Psalm 36:8b). They have the opportunity to drink of the river of delights.

Fourth, God is portrayed as a fountain of life (Psalm 36:9a). Those who come and drink of Him have perpetual life. He is our source of eternal life, our neverending supply of living water.

Fifth, God is described as light (Psalm 36:9b). Those who come will have light and will truly be able to see. As a flashlight provides light for our physical eyes, God provides light for our spiritual eyes. The words "light" and "life" speak of the fullness of salvation and an understanding of what it means to be in the presence of God.

What an array of significant terms: "life-giver," "house," "river," "fountain," and "light"! Together they suggest that the Lord, the Source of all wisdom and love, will grant His children all our needs.

These scenes remind us of the Garden of Eden, where man enjoyed a paradise. The bliss of Eden may be experienced again in a righteous fellowship with God.

When someone asks, "Do you believe in life after death?" he has asked the wrong question. What should be asked is "Do you believe in the faithfulness of God?" God has clearly told us what He will do about all the tomorrows of those who trust in Him. Thus only one question needs to be asked: "Will God keep His promises?" If the answer to that question is "Yes!" then there is a glorious life beyond the grave!

*The Christian looks at God as the
all-sufficient God. With Him we have
everything; without Him we have nothing
of real importance. With Him we are rich
indeed; without Him we are paupers.*

*In prayer, praise God for the riches
that you enjoy in His house.*

24

GOD AND THE ETERNAL NOW

*"God said to Moses, 'I AM WHO I AM'; and
He said, 'Thus you shall say to the sons of Israel,
"I AM has sent me to you"'" (Exodus 3:14).*

*"But do not let this one fact escape your
notice, beloved, that with the Lord one day is like
a thousand years, and a thousand years like one
day" (2 Peter 3:8).*

God lives in the eternal now. For this reason, He
is the God of the past, the present, and the future. He
has worked, does work, and will work.

The past is full of His wonders. Surveying the past
is encouraging to the child of God because such a
survey reminds us that God has always been providentially watching over us. We usually see more looking
back on our days than we ever saw when we were
living them.

Indeed, we have a history with God. We have

prayed, and He has answered us. We have come to Him for forgiveness, and He has granted it. We have sought His wisdom, and He has given it. He has providentially watched over us as a faithful father cares for his children. Who can forget what God did for us yesterday?

The present is full of His thoughts and actions. God is active now—thinking gracious thoughts toward us and working His will in our lives. He works in plain sight and behind the scenes to achieve His divine purposes in concert with mankind's free moral agency. If the curtain were pulled back and we were allowed to see what God does for us, we would be overwhelmed.

Jesus came into this world to be Immanuel, or "God with us." God is transcendent, but He is never far away. Christ walked among the candlesticks in Revelation 1, symbolizing that He was with His followers in the furnace of affliction. Thus those who know Him can hug to their hearts the wonderful truth that if His children must walk in the fires of trial, He will walk in those fires with them.

The future is full of His plans. He holds our future in His hands. When we get to the tomorrows of this earth that lie ahead, if there are such, we will find that God has lived in them also and has cleared away the debris to make smooth the road we must travel in them. Jesus had John the Immerser leveling the hills and filling in the valleys for Him; and we have Jesus and the almighty God going before us, defending us, preparing the way for us, and getting the future ready for us.

As we squint our eyes and look at what is coming, we can only characterize it with one word—God. He will bless us tomorrow, save us tomorrow, mature us tomorrow, and introduce us to heaven tomorrow. Think of all His plans that are yet to be fulfilled!

God sees and meets all our needs—those that arise from the past, the difficulties of the present, and the ones that glare at us from the high perch of the future. He has made provisions to heal our past, He walks with us now, and He guarantees a beautiful tomorrow.

No human being can say that he or she is not surrounded by God—God is in our past, our present, and our future. We have lived, moved, and breathed through Him, and we will do so today and throughout all the future that awaits us.

The infinitude of God does not allow Him to live in the past. He lives in the eternal now, looking down on eternity past, the present moment, and eternity future.

In prayer, praise God that He holds your time in His hands. You cannot handle the past, present, or the future; but God can.

25

A New Song of Praise

> *"I waited patiently for the Lord; and He inclined to me and heard my cry"; "He put a new song in my mouth, a song of praise to our God; many will see and fear and will trust in the Lord"* (Psalm 40:1, 3).

> *"To Him who loves us and released us from our sins by His blood—and He has made us to be a kingdom, priests to His God and Father—to Him be the glory and the dominion forever and ever. Amen"* (Revelation 1:5b, 6).

If one does not remember all that God has done for him, he will not praise Him. However, looking back on His kind deeds will remind us of His goodness and will put a song of praise on our lips. Re-read the history book of your life, and then write a new song about His mercy!

He has heard our prayers. Surely all of us who trust in Him can glance back over the years and see where God has answered our prayers. We have prayed, and God has bent low and heard our halting petitions.

He has rescued us from destruction. As we scan the pages of the past, we can see where God has lifted us out of the miry pit of destruction. Perhaps we were slipping over the brink into the hellish pit of sin and God lifted us out, rescuing us from the greedy fingers of the devil. Maybe we were approaching the door of death through a sickness or an accident and God pulled us back and gave us new life. Innumerable times we have been saved by the mercy of God.

He has put our feet on solid ground. We can see that God has given us firm footing so that we can serve Him once again. He has put us on a level place so that we can do His will and fulfill His plan.

These wondrous deeds of kindness have given us a new song. His grace to us and His great acts of love should put a new song in our hearts and on our lips. If we do not have a happy song of deliverance to sing, we simply have not looked carefully at all the ways we have been blessed.

Do what the psalmist did. Do what John asked us to do. Stop and look back at what God has done for you. His hand of grace has been upon your life, and seeing it will set your soul to singing of His wonderful love and enduring mercy.

When Jeremiah had almost nothing to rejoice in, he said, "The Lord's lovingkindnesses indeed never cease, for His compassions never fail. They are new every morning; great is Your faithfulness" (Lamentations 3:22, 23). When we get to heaven, we will have no trouble singing a new song of victory.

> "And they sang a new song, saying, 'Worthy are You . . . for You were slain, and purchased for God with Your blood men from every tribe and tongue and people and nation. You have made them to be a kingdom and priests to our God" (Revelation 5:9, 10a).

As we prepare for that great song-fest before His throne, let us practice, tuning our hearts and lips by looking at God's goodness and composing a new song of praise here.

The songs of the world are usually pitiful songs because the people of the world have nothing to sing about. The Christian has a new song, a song that is new every morning because He has seen God's grace and love in his life afresh.

In prayer, praise God for His faithfulness.

26

WONDERS TOO NUMEROUS TO COUNT

"Many, O Lord my God, are the wonders which You have done, and Your thoughts toward us; there is none to compare with You. If I would declare and speak them, they would be too numerous to count" (Psalm 40:5).

"Are not two sparrows sold for a cent? And yet not one of them will fall to the ground apart from your Father. But the very hairs of your head are all numbered. So do not fear; you are more valuable than many sparrows" (Matthew 10:29–31).

As we review the actions of God toward His people, we are able to reach some important conclusions about His nature.

First, He has blessed all who trust in Him. There are no exceptions. He has never forsaken any of His trusting children. He has never broken a covenant or violated a promise; He speaks words that are faithful and true.

Second, His deeds are not only kind but also gracious. Kind deeds are generous deeds, but *gracious* deeds are undeserved deeds. He has loved His people when they did not deserve loving.

When we were down and out and away from God, thoughtless and indifferent, He sought us, found us, and brought us back to His fold as a loving shepherd. He has always given us what we have needed, not what we have deserved.

Third, He is full of gracious thoughts toward His people. His gracious actions were spawned by gracious thoughts. His compassionate heart has guided His tender hand.

Sometimes we say to one another, "What are you thinking?" We know that the one to whom we are speaking may be thinking an erroneous thought about us. How comforting it is to realize that God is always thinking good, noble, and gracious thoughts about His people!

Fourth, His deeds of grace are continuous and innumerable. These deeds have been unending. There have been so many of them that we could not count them if we really tried. Everywhere we look, we see the hand of God. He has surrounded those who trust in Him with gifts of His faithfulness.

How great our God is! His power transcends our frail ability to comprehend, but so does His grace. It goes out to all, reaches down to the worst, and will lift anyone who receives it all the way to heaven. His wonders are inconceivable, innumerable, and impartial. He loves us with a love that is stronger than death, a love that will not let us go.

*When we contemplate God's grace
and goodness we become lost in the wonder
and depth of it all. We count on His deeds
of kindness, but they are too numerous
for us to count. We can enjoy them,
but we cannot enumerate them.*

*In prayer, praise God for His storehouse
of riches to which He has given you a key.*

27

THINKING ON GOD'S LOVINGKINDNESS

"We have thought on Your lovingkindness, O God, in the midst of Your temple" (Psalm 48:9).

"Being justified as a gift by His grace through the redemption which is in Christ Jesus (Romans 3:24).

The big word, the word of grace and glory, in the Old Testament is "lovingkindness." Anyone who claims that there is no grace in the Old Testament has not encountered this grace-and-loyalty-filled word.

The first truth about this word is that it points us to God's nature. That He will answer those who come to Him with lovingkindness and not according to their sins is seen throughout Psalms and the New Testament. The New Testament says that God is love, but the Old Testament says that God is full of loving-kindness.

The second truth about lovingkindness is that it is constant. He is not capricious, having one type of character one day and a different kind the next day. He is the same—yesterday, today, and forever. He does not waver. In Him, there is no shadow of turning. This fact does not mean that He will not judge sin; it means that lovingkindness is His continual nature toward anyone who puts his or her obedient trust in Him.

This word is greater than our minds can conceive. Try as we might, we cannot fully digest it. It reaches to the heavens, the psalmist says. As we contemplate it, we find that it is greater and far more amazing than our brains can comprehend, and we become lost in the mystery, magnitude, and marvel of it.

How wonderful it is to think about God's covenant loyalty! It gives us confidence, assurance, and boldness in our relationship with Him.

The most abiding certainty that God has given us is this: When we trust in Him we will find that we are surrounded by His lovingkindness.

In prayer, praise God for His everlasting and ever-present lovingkindness.

28

THE QUIET WORKINGS OF GOD

> *"O God, we have heard with our ears, our fathers have told us the work that You did in their days, in the days of old" (Psalm 44:1).*

> *"For He Himself has said, 'I will never desert you, nor will I ever forsake you'" (Hebrews 13:5b).*

One of our big questions about God comes from deep within us: "How does God work?" However, who can answer such a question fully? He is the almighty, eternal God; He is incomprehensible, omnipresent, and immutable! Nevertheless, some truths have been revealed in the Scriptures regarding His divine workings.

He has worked miraculously. The writer of Psalm 44 was concerned that his generation had not seen God's miracles. His forefathers had spoken to them about the miraculous works they had seen, but the writer and his people had not seen such divine demonstrations. They were wondering why.

He has worked non-miraculously. A truth that comes out in this psalm is that His power was not always miraculously demonstrated in Old and New Testament times. Sometimes He chose to reveal His strength in quiet, behind-the-scenes ways.

For example, God did not rescue baby Moses from among the reeds in the Nile by a miracle; He did it with His providential oversight. He worked within the realm of nature, using Pharaoh's daughter to preserve Moses and give him the training needed for him to lead Israel out of bondage. Israel did not know what God was doing until eighty years later. We could call this action on God's part "His silent workings."

Today, in a way beyond our understanding, He works in our behalf through His providence—through both His silent and visible providence. His providing for us does not set aside the laws of nature, as His confirming miracles did in Old and New Testament days. Rather, He works within the laws of nature and sometimes causes one law to supercede another. Perhaps His providence today is not as flashy, direct, and confronting as were His miraculous signs in olden times. However, He moves today with His same great power, caring for us by performing His wonders.

Psalm 44 highlights the miracles that God worked in the past. It does not mention His providence per se, but it implies His providence in verses 2 and 3. The sweeping descriptions that are mentioned—"then You planted them" and "then You spread them aboard"— suggest God's visible and silent actions in behalf of His people. Bringing Israel into a land which had standing grain that was ripe and ready for them to eat (Joshua 5:12) is an example of God's care over His nation. Assuredly, behind the scenes, undetected by the human eye and mind, were the providential workings of God.

At times He may seemingly say no to our prayers, but—invisible to us—He moves quietly to accomplish His will in behalf of what is best for His children. Belief in the fact of God's quiet workings is a big part of what it means to walk by faith (2 Corinthians 5:7).

When we cannot see God's actions,
we can trust His heart and confidently believe
that He is silently working behind
the physical veil of what we see.

In prayer, praise God for His great
providence, in which He reveals both
His silent and His visible workings.

29

GOD'S GIFT OF THE HOME

> "Wives, be subject to your own husbands, as to the Lord. For the husband is the head of the wife, as Christ also is the head of the church, He Himself being the Savior of the body"; "Husbands, love your wives, just as Christ also loved the church and gave Himself up for her" (Ephesians 5:22, 23, 25).

The couple who has brought to their marriage God's design for the home will find it easy to praise God for the home. This beautiful relationship that is to be patterned after the sacred picture described in Ephesians 5 will be a haven of love and a foretaste of glory divine.

The husband is the head. One of William Shakespeare's characters in the play *Much Ado About Nothing* stated that if two men ride the same horse at the same time, one will have to ride behind. This practical truth applies to marriage. God has put a leader of the home in His blueprint for the family.

The husband is commanded to lead in the home—in sacrificial love, as Christ loved the church (Ephesians 5:25). The wife is commanded to follow his leadership in loving submission that is as unto the Lord (Ephesians 5:22).

The wife is the queen. She provides the heart of the home. The wife does not take center stage in this Ephesian passage, but she is acknowledged as a beautiful centerpiece, without which the home has no soul. The bridegroom has wooed her, he has won her, and she has given him her heart. They stand side by side as a wonderful social unit, each complementing the other. They are two, but they are one. They walk together, though he is the head and she is the heart.

God provides the map and the guidance of the home. Only when the husband and the wife live to honor God's will do they find the meaning, the peace, and the future that they seek for their marriage. Through God's map, the home develops spiritual roots that will hold it together through the trials, difficulties, and burdens that life brings.

God's design provides for our happiness and for the proper ordering of the home. Obedience to His plan is the avenue to marital success. Deviations from His instructions, whether through ignorance or rebellion, bring only frustration and regrets.

The home is God's gift to mankind and to the social

order of the earth. Who could imagine our world without the home? Two extremely significant affirmations from God are given to us at the beginning of the Bible: "Let us make man in Our image" (Genesis 1:26) and "I will make him a helper suitable for him" (Genesis 2:18). Resulting from these two announcements was the home, about which the Spirit said, "A man . . . and his wife . . . shall become one flesh." The union of a man and a woman in marriage forms the single most important and beautiful social unit of the human race (Genesis 2:24).

We must add to all these truths the advent of Jesus. When Christ came, He hallowed and sanctified the home, making it an even more treasured haven of peace and love. Let us give thanks and praise to God for His wonderful gift of the home.

If Christ lives in the home, the home becomes heaven on earth, the sweetest place known to us. If Christ does not live in it, the home can become a horrible jumble of discontented people, a place where pain and misery abound.

In prayer, praise God for the heaven-like Christian home that He has given to the sons and daughters of Adam.

30

"Nothing Good Will I Withhold"

> *"But they who seek the Lord shall not be in want of any good thing" (Psalm 34:10b).*

> *"I came that they may have life, and have it abundantly" (John 10:10b).*

The amazing promise of Psalm 34:10b and John 10:10b, that God will give the believer a full and complete life, is one of the most sweeping promises of the entire Bible. Coupled with a condition, it is given as an encouragement to God's faithful children, not to the unbeliever or the disobedient person.

God gave us this promise to cherish, and it is appropriate for us to ask, "Is it always true? How shall we understand or interpret His promise?" Perhaps the best way to grasp it is to look at the life of Jesus. He is the perfect illustration of how God carries out His loving care for His people.

In light of how God cared for Jesus, we can say that this promise is a promise about responsible care. God will not satisfy our vain greeds, but He will meet our true needs. He has never allowed any child of His to experience the loss of the actual help that is needed. No "truly good thing" will be withheld from him.

We can see that it is a promise that is more about spiritual sustenance than physical security. Jesus received God's gracious benefits, but He never lived in a palace. His needs were always met, but He never had an abundance of money. From the viewpoint of the world, He lived without luxury and conveniences; but from the observation of heaven, He was blessed with the gold of God.

We see that it is a promise that God will keep within the confines of His eternal purposes. He will not throw away His plan for all people in order to satisfy the wants or wishes of a few. In our homes, we do not sacrifice the other family members' needs for the desires of one. Likewise, it is clear from Gethsemane that God makes the needs of all the people of the world His chief concern. He has to consider the needs of His other children as He ministers to ours.

We see that it is a promise that will be carried out in the midst of afflictions. In Psalm 34:19 the warning is given that the righteous will face many "afflictions." In other words, the promise does not preclude difficulties. The promise is that God will sustain the righteous in, or will deliver the righteous from, the afflictions that come.

Jesus was crucified for our sins, but God supplied strength for Him at His chosen hour. God has allowed some of His people to be offered as sacrifices on the martyr's altar, but behind the dim unknown He sustained them. He provided for their real needs during their darkest hours. Through their examples, He provided for His other children by giving them inspiration and courage to be faithful until the end. Neither the martyr nor those who needed the example were deprived of what they really needed.

Behind this wonderful promise must be placed trust in our heavenly Father's wisdom and knowledge. He will faithfully keep His promise according to His wise judgments and our best interests.

Anyone hidden in God through Christ
has all that he needs—the provisions
of His grace, the protection of His
great arm, the power of His Word,
and the personal presence of His Son.

In prayer, praise God for the absolute,
complete care that He provides for His own.

31

IN THE THICK OF BATTLE

"... 'I come to you in the name of the Lord of hosts, the God of the armies of Israel, whom you have taunted. This day the Lord will deliver you up into my hands, ... that all the earth may know that there is a God in Israel'" (1 Samuel 17:45, 46).

"The Lord will rescue me from every evil deed, and will bring me safely to His heavenly kingdom; to Him be the glory forever and ever. Amen" (2 Timothy 4:18).

As we go forth to battle, as we wage the war with the prince of darkness, we go with the praises of God in our hearts and on our lips. One uniqueness about us, one dominate feature of our character, is our commitment to give glory and adoration to God even in the thick of battle.

David went before Goliath with five smooth stones; but when he spoke of what he was doing, he did not hold up the stones—he held up his true Rock, Yahweh, his God! He said to Goliath, "You come to me with a sword, a spear, and a javelin, but I come to you in the name of the Lord of hosts, the God of the armies of Israel . . ." (1 Samuel 17:45). The most conspicuous part of David's battle plan was God.

What Samson could not do with miraculous might for the nation of Israel, *Samuel* did with consecration to God in prayer. Amazingly, before Samuel led the people to war, he conducted a revival. Before they sharpened their swords, they offered sacrifices to God, with confession and supplication (1 Samuel 7:10). The clearest thing about Samuel's leadership was his reliance on God.

Jehoshaphat was destined to confront the Moabites, Ammonites, and Meunites in a great battle (2 Chronicles 20:1). The army that opposed him was vast, well-armed, strong, skilled, and intimidating. He gathered his nation before God and asked Him to deliver them. In the midst of that assembly, Jahaziel the prophet said that they would receive the victory without raising a sword (2 Chronicles 20:14–17). Jehoshaphat told the nation to trust in the Lord and they would see success. He sent the priests ahead of his army, singing, "Give thanks to the Lord, for His lovingkindness is everlasting" (2 Chronicles 20:21). When they arrived at the battlefield, the enemy had already been defeated by the Lord. No one can miss the place of praise in this victory.

It has been said that all great spiritual battles are won the day before in the closet of prayer. Great leaders are led by the Lord. They have gone out to do God's will, praising Him. They have gone in His name, in His strength, and for His glory.

All our victories are surrounded with the glory, grace, and grandeur of the Lord. The battle is won with songs of praise that acknowledge, lift up, and give thanks for God's leadership and the magnitude of His will. It is never won with swords of the flesh or with human wisdom.

> Thus says the Lord, "Let not a wise man boast of his wisdom, and let not the mighty man boast of his might, let not a rich man boast of his riches; but let him who boasts boast of this, that he understands and knows Me, that I am the Lord who exercises lovingkindness, justice and righteousness on earth; for I delight in these things," declares the Lord (Jeremiah 9:23, 24).

As you check your quiver, make sure that you have the arrow of praise in it.

In prayer, praise God for all the victories that He has given us: the big ones, the little ones, and all the ones in between.

32

GOD'S GLORY IN US

*"Great is the Lord, and greatly to be praised.
. . . Beautiful in elevation, the joy of the whole
earth, is Mount Zion in the far north. . . ."; "As
is Your name, O God, so is Your praise to the
ends of the earth" (Psalm 48:1, 2, 10a).*

*". . . you have been bought with a price:
therefore glorify God in your body" (1 Corinthians 6:20).*

*"That He would grant you, according to the
riches of His glory, to be strengthened with
power through His Spirit in the inner man"
(Ephesians 3:16).*

Yahweh, the King of His people, should be praised
continually. Four elements of His greatness are de-
tected in Psalm 48:1, 2, and 10 and in the prayer of Paul
in Ephesians 3:16.

He gives significance to those who put their faith in

Him. God stands above and beyond all other kings because He brings to His people worth and meaning. Jerusalem would have been just another city, but God's choice to put His name on it made it the greatest of all cities. The writer of Psalm 48 said of Jerusalem because of God's touch of grace, "Beautiful in elevation, the joy of the whole earth" (v. 2a).

He beautifies whatever He touches. He took Jerusalem, an average-looking city, and made it the envy of the nations of the world. He brought glory and holiness to it. God's glory flows out to those who have close proximity to Him.

He is the believer's stronghold. Those who trust in Him find Him to be their citadel of strength, a fortress of power. They are safe from all enemies—not because of their human military prowess, their wisdom, or their acumen, but because God is with them. He has never failed His people. The kings of the earth looked at Jerusalem and fled in terror because they knew whose hand shielded it (v. 5).

He brings gladness to His people. As they feel the warmth and comfort of His providence and provisions, their hearts break into rejoicing. As a consequence, a confident joy resides in their souls.

One of the most natural things for the faithful child of God to do is to praise Him, for He is his great King. His greatness is unparalleled. He beautifies the place where He dwells. He is the refuge of His people, filling the trusting heart with confidence during the toughest parts of life.

If we do not have true beauty, it is because the beauty of God is not falling upon us.

In prayer, praise God for the glory that He shares with all who live in Him.

33

"Who Is the King of Glory?"

> *"Lift up your heads, O gates, and be lifted up, O ancient doors, that the King of glory may come in! Who is the King of glory? The Lord strong and mighty, the Lord mighty in battle. . . . Who is this King of glory? The Lord of hosts, He is the King of glory. Selah" (Psalm 24:7–10).*

> *"Yet I will exult in the Lord, I will rejoice in the God of my salvation. The Lord God is my strength, and He has made my feet like hinds' feet, and makes me walk on my high places" (Habakkuk 3:18, 19).*

The question "Who is the King of glory?" is asked twice in Psalm 24:7–10. The answer is given in Habakkuk 3:18, 19a and scattered throughout the Scriptures.

He is the Creator of all things. Without Him nothing was made that has been made (Genesis 1:1). Through Jesus, God brought everything into existence; and with His hand of power, He sustains all existing things. One day, at the time of His choosing, He will give us a new heaven and a new earth (2 Peter 3:13). In Christ all things have the potential of being reconciled to God. "By the word of the Lord the heavens were made, and by the breath of His mouth all their host"; "Let all the earth fear the Lord; let all the inhabitants of the world stand in awe of Him. For He spoke, and it was done; He commanded, and it stood fast" (Psalm 33:6, 8, 9).

He is the Good Shepherd over those who trust in Him. He provides for us—giving the sustenance and rest we require (Psalm 23:1). His provisions are laid before us in the midst of an evil and vicious world: "He prepares a table before us in the presence of our enemies" (Psalm 23:5).

He is the invincible, mighty Warrior for His people. He goes before us into every battle we must fight (Psalm 18:7–15). His strong hand delivers us from every foe.

He is the Lord Almighty for whom nothing is too hard. He can deliver us from every trial and strengthen us for every victory (Psalm 121:5–8). He stands above time with all power, guiding unerringly, and lovingly watching over His own.

To stand in the presence of this glorious One is the greatest experience that a human being can know. He is the great and mighty, glorious and transcendent

Lord. May all creatures of the earth bow down and acknowledge Him as the true God!

We cannot give true thanks to God unless
we know who God is and what He has done!

In prayer, worship the only true and living
God, the almighty One, who holds
the universe in the palm of His hand
and who holds us as the apple of His eye.

34

THE JOY OF GOD

"How blessed are all who take refuge in Him!" (Psalm 2:12c).

"Rejoice in the Lord always; again I will say, rejoice!" (Philippians 4:4).

In the early part of the Book of Psalms, the word "blessed" appears eight times (1:1; 2:12; 32:1, 2; 33:12; 34:8; 40:4; 41:1). When these passages are traced out, we see the pathway to true happiness, the roadway to the joy of the Lord.

Happiness comes from being a righteous person (Psalm 1:1). This beatitude is presented in a negative statement—by affirming what the righteous person does not do. He does not walk, stand, or sit with the wicked. It reminds us of our Lord's words: "Blessed are the pure in heart" (Matthew 5:8a); "Blessed are those who hunger and thirst for righteousness, for they shall be satisfied" (Matthew 5:6).

Happiness comes from finding refuge in God (Psalms 2:12; 34:8). This beatitude mentioned in two psalms highlights the man who allows God to be his shield. He comes to God and asks Him to be his fortress, defense, and stronghold. Perhaps this promise is similar to our Lord's beatitudes: "Blessed are the poor in spirit, for theirs is the kingdom of heaven" (Matthew 5:3); "Blessed are those who have been persecuted for the sake of righteousness" (Matthew 5:10a).

Happiness is enjoying forgiveness (Psalm 32:1, 2). The word "blessed" is used twice in these two verses, but forgiveness is emphasized in each case. There is simply no peace without forgiveness. One might say that this beatitude is about making peace with God and with others—somewhat like, "Blessed are the peacemakers, for they shall be called sons of God" (Matthew 5:9).

Happiness is being a nation under God (Psalm 33:12). No nation can find true prosperity, peace, and success unless it lives and rules under God's leadership. This beatitude would be the only one of the eight that admonishes a community. This congratulation hints at another beatitude: "Blessed are the gentle, for they shall inherit the earth" (Matthew 5:5).

Happiness is trusting in the Lord Psalm (40:4). Life can be miserable unless one is living by faith in God. He who puts his confidence in anything in this world is headed for a tragic disappointment. God gives us stability, and through His stability we find peace.

Happiness is considering the weak (Psalm 41:1). One cannot find the peace of God unless he is treating others right. This beatitude has to do with a heart of compassion. It is a blessing that is in line with our Lord's beatitude: "Blessed are the merciful, for they shall receive mercy" (Matthew 5:7).

When these beatitudes are combined, we have a beautiful picture of how a godly person is to live. Having this lifestyle not only brings a life of harmony with God's will; but it also guides one into the good life of prosperity, peace, and happiness.

*Joy is always a consequence, never
a conquest; it is the fruit, not the root.*

*In prayer, praise God for showing us the way
to true happiness in this life.*

35

GOD'S AMAZING LOVE

"Blessed be the Lord, for He has made marvelous His lovingkindness to me in a besieged city"; "O love the Lord, all you His godly ones! The Lord preserves the faithful . . ." (Psalm 31:21, 23).

"Then some children were brought to Him so that He might lay His hands on them and pray; and the disciples rebuked them. But Jesus said, 'Let the children alone, and do not hinder them from coming to Me; for the kingdom of heaven belongs to such as these.' After laying His hands on them, He departed from there" (Matthew 19:13–15).

"The one who does not love does not know God, for God is love" (1 John 4:8).

Verses 21 and 23 of Psalm 31 comprise a short doxology that extols God's loving nature. The writer remembered that God had protected him when he was within a besieged city. This remembering of God's goodness had inspired him to praise Him. Add to this doxology Matthew 19:14 and 1 John 4:8, and contemplate the great love with which He has loved us.

He loves us in word. Over and over again, in eloquent and picturesque language, God tells of the love that He has for us. Every book of the Bible declares in some form His great affection for all people and especially for His children.

He loves us in deed. His love does not end with words—He has continually demonstrated it in the highest and most positive ways. John urged Christians to make sure that they do not love just in word or tongue but in deed and truth (1 John 3:18). God is the perfect example of "love-in-action" for Christians to follow. His deliverances, His meeting our needs, and His providing for our salvation through His Son speak of His affection for us.

He loves us in faithfulness. His love is continuous and unrelenting. In a world of uncertainty, one truth that we can always stand on is God's amazing love. The writer of Psalm 31 reached a time when he thought he was cut off from God, but shortly thereafter God answered his prayer: "As for me, I said in my alarm, 'I am cut off from before Your eyes'; nevertheless You heard the voice of my supplications when I cried to You" (Psalm 31:22). In this way, He reminds us that we should never conclude that God has forsaken us.

The believer spends much of his life rejoicing in the love God has for him. He remembers it, lives in it, and looks forward to it.

Could we with ink the ocean fill,
  And were the sky of parchment made;
Were ev'ry stalk on earth a quill,
  And ev'ry man a scribe by trade;
To write the love of God above
  Would drain the ocean dry;
Nor could the scroll contain the whole
  Tho stretched from sky to sky.
                    —*F. M. Lehman*

In prayer, praise God for His wonderful love for this world of people, especially for His people and the little children.

36

THE VISION OF WORSHIP

"In the year of King Uzziah's death I saw the Lord sitting on a throne, lofty and exalted, with the train of His robe filling the temple"; "Then I heard the voice of the Lord, saying, 'Whom shall I send, and who will go for Us?' Then I said, 'Here am I. Send me!'" (Isaiah 6:1, 8).

"Cease striving and know that I am God; I will be exalted among the nations, I will be exalted in the earth" (Psalm 46:10).

"It is a trustworthy statement, deserving full acceptance, that Christ Jesus came into the world to save sinners. . . ."; "Now to the King eternal, immortal, invisible, the only God, be honor and glory forever and ever. Amen" (1 Timothy 1:15, 17).

While at the temple, Isaiah was given a majestic, supernatural vision of God. He said, "I saw the Lord sitting on a throne, lofty and exalted, with the train of

His robe filling the temple" (Isaiah 6:1).

What do we see when we are worshiping God? Admittedly, we should not expect a miraculous, prophetic revelation as Isaiah received, but true worship should open our eyes to God's multicolored attributes.

Two men were walking out of a worship service. One said, "Wasn't he a great preacher!" while the other said, "Don't we have a great God!" The writer of this psalm, like the second man, saw the greatness of God in his worship.

As he worshiped, he saw God's past mercies. He thought of the walk that he had experienced with God, and that reminded him of how gracious God had been to him. Can we sing about God without thinking about what He has done for us?

As he worshiped, he saw God's power. Thinking of God immediately brings to mind His might and His indescribable strength. We can easily say what the angel said to Abraham: "Is anything too difficult for the Lord?" (Genesis 18:14a).

As he worshiped, he saw God's glory. God is a glorious God. To be sure, His glory far exceeds any glory man can imagine. In Isaiah's vision, the glory of the Lord filled the temple (Isaiah 6:1). When one truly worships, he is bathed in God's greatness, and his soul is filled with His glory.

Worship, then, goes in and up: From our hearts and lips, it goes up to God as sweet-smelling sacrifices and it also remains with us, filling our souls with renewed images of the character and attributes of God. As we bring our gifts of praise to Him, we behold His glory and are transformed by it, from worship service to worship service, from glory to glory (2 Corinthians 3:18).

*The greatest vision you will ever have
is when you see God in His love and power
in your worship of Him.*

*In prayer, praise God for His divine glory,
strength, and mercy that we see
each time we worship Him.*

37

"For Such Is God"

"For such is God, our God forever and ever; He will guide us until death" (Psalm 48:14).

"It is a trustworthy statement: for if we died with Him, we will also live with Him; if we endure, we will also reign with Him" (2 Timothy 2:11, 12a).

What kind of nature does God have? He is full of lovingkindness. Psalm 48:14 looks at this side of God's character from the standpoint of His leadership of those who trust in Him. How does He walk with His people?

God takes us up. This part of the promise is an implication. When we are down and out, He pulls us up and takes us on as His personal project. We come to Him in faith and obedience, and God adopts us as His children of grace. He says, "As long as you follow Me with love and devotion, I will be responsible for you.

I will see that you have all that you need to do My will" (see Matthew 6:33).

He continually guides us. The verb that is used suggests continuation. The idea is "I will be among you, constantly guiding you." God Himself, with His Word and His fellowship, will be our compass.

He promises to be with us until the end. The word "death" is in the text, and it points to the end of our journey here. The promise is that God will be with us until we have gone through the wilderness of this world and made our exit into His presence. God will stay with us until the journey is completed and we have safely arrived in His celestial house.

He is the eternal God. He will never drift into someone's life and give a momentary push and then disappear. He comes in to stay—to take us up, to guide us by walking beside us, and to see that we have made it safely to His side in His Golden City of eternal life.

God through His Son has saved us,
and God through His Son will keep us
saved if we hold on to Him.
He who has begun a redeeming work
in us will complete it to His glory.

In prayer, praise God for saving us
and keeping us saved.

38

WORSHIP AND WORRY

"You caused judgment to be heard from heaven; the earth feared and was still when God arose to judgment, to save all the humble of the earth. Selah" (Psalm 76:8, 9).

". . . do not be worried about your life, as to what you will eat or what you will drink; nor for your body, as to what you will put on"; "For your heavenly Father knows that you need all these things" (Matthew 6:25a, 32b).

"Be anxious for nothing, but in everything by prayer and supplication with thanksgiving let your requests be made known to God" (Philippians 4:6).

Although Psalm 76 is only twelve verses long, it is graphic in its picture of God. Let us allow this description to guide us into a deeper appreciation of who God is; and, with this view of God, let us allow it to banish our fears. Before we worry about our circumstances, let us worship the great God we serve. We will find that our worship gives our worries wings, making them fly away into oblivion.

We see in this psalm that God is the God who is near. The psalmist wrote, "God is known in Judah; His name is great in Israel. His tabernacle is in Salem; His dwelling place also is in Zion" (vv. 1, 2). Salem stands for Jerusalem. God dwelt in that city among His people. He ruled the world, but He also lived among the nation He had chosen. He is transcendent and immanent, as the scholar would say. He is not the God who sits on a distant star; He is the God who dwelt in Salem. In the New Testament we are told, "If anyone loves Me, he will keep My word; and My Father will love him, and We will come to him and make Our abode with him" (John 14:23). The Christian has the bracing assurance that God and Christ dwell within him. He can say with the psalmist that God is near.

Furthermore, we are assured by these words that He is the divine Warrior. This image is the basic picture of the psalm. "At Your rebuke, O God of Jacob, both rider and horse were cast into a dead sleep" (v. 6). Could this description be a figurative depiction of Sennacherib's arrogant encircling of Jerusalem? The writer's poetic words remind us that when His people are in trouble, God triumphs over the ones disturbing them. With only a blink of His eye, He turns even the wrath of man into a chorus of praise to His greatness. If need be, God will use nature or pagans to accomplish His will and protect His own.

It is implied that He is the universal King. The psalm says, "The earth feared and was still when God arose to judgment, to save all the humble of the earth" (vv. 8b, 9). His kind providence extends to the far reaches of the land, making all the humble of the earth His subjects. He ruled Israel to be sure, but His rulership also encompassed the earth. Because of the width of His reign, the kings of the earth fear Him. No land is too distant, no island is too obscure, no country is too immense to be beyond the reach of His rule.

We are taught that He is the eternal Judge. "You caused judgment to be heard from heaven; the earth feared and was still" (v. 8). Since God is the only true God, He is the only true Judge. His judgment is immediate and distant; He judges us now and will judge us tomorrow. He judged Sennacherib, king of Assyria, to manifest who He is and His concern for His people. The earth saw His judgments and stood in awe. At the time of His choosing, He will bring all people before Him for a final reckoning. Every human being will give an account to this God who made him and rules over him.

Who, then, is God? He is the God who dwells among His people, He is the divine and holy Warrior, He is the universal King, and He is the eternal Judge.

Can one understand who God is and not wish to bow before Him in sacred worship? When we realize who God is, we ask ourselves anew, "Why should I worry about anything?"

If God is the God the Bible pictures Him to be, if Jesus is the Savior of man that the Scriptures say He is, and you have the right relationship with God through Christ, is there ever a need for you to worry?

In prayer, praise God for the privilege of living a life that is free from worry.

39

"HE KEEPS US IN LIFE"

"Bless our God, . . . who keeps us in life and does not allow our feet to slip" (Psalm 66:8, 9).

"For in Him we live and move and exist" (Acts 17:28a).

"[For you,] who are protected by the power of God through faith for a salvation ready to be revealed in the last time" (1 Peter 1:5).

The writer of Psalm 66 said that God is the One who "keeps us in life" (v. 9). This was his poetical way of saying that God had kept His servants alive. He had protected them from death.

We can say something similar regarding our spiritual lives. He sustains us spiritually and physically. He has raised us up from death and put us in Christ (Ephesians 2:5), giving us new life and lavishing upon us all spiritual blessings (Ephesians 1:3). Furthermore, He renews the Christian's life each day.

How does He bring all of this about?

By forgiveness. We enjoy a constant cleansing of sin. As our physical blood cleanses our bodies, even so the precious blood of Jesus keeps us clean in Christ (1 John 1:7). He has not only saved us, but He also keeps us saved and justified in His sight.

Through fellowship. Our brethren revive us spiritually by encouraging us, rebuking us, and teaching us. We are surrounded by a great cloud of witnesses who have gone before us (Hebrews 12:1). They inspire and encourage us by their examples. In the present world, we have a great assembly of brothers and sisters who are going along with us as we journey to our eternal home. We exhort our fellow Christians and provoke one another to love and good deeds (Hebrews 10:24).

With the guidance of His Word. His words are the words of life because they impart life, strength, character, and hope (Philippians 2:16). They are energized by the Holy Spirit. His Word is our source of life and our sustenance in life; we are led and fed by it. We hold fast the word of life (Philippians 2:16), and we hold it forth for others to see and receive.

Through the awareness of His presence. Our consciousness that God is in us and with us causes us to look at our power and not at our problems—at our strengths, not at our struggles. Through His glorious presence we are more than conquerors in this life.

Others may forsake us, but the Lord will stand with us and strengthen us to the very end (2 Timothy 4:17).

When we look at what we have in Christ, we say to ourselves with amazement, "How abundant is the life in Christ! Surely those who do not know Him do not know what they are missing." This life that we have is not a life that results from positive thinking. It is given and sustained by God Himself! Let us praise God, the One who keeps us in life!

God through His Son is the author of all life;
He gives all of the physical life and
the spiritual life we have in Christ.
Remember the words of John:
"In Him was life, and the life
was the Light of men" (John 1:4).

In prayer, praise God for His giving us the
rich, royal life in His Son and keeping us in it.

40

"There Let Us Rejoice In Him!"

"Come and see the works of God, who is awesome in His deeds toward the sons of men. He turned the sea into dry land; they passed through the river on foot; there let us rejoice in Him!"; "Bless our God, O peoples, and sound His praise abroad" (Psalm 66:5, 6, 8).

"When the angels had gone away from them into heaven, the shepherds began saying to one another, 'Let us go straight to Bethlehem then, and see this thing that has happened which the Lord has made known to us'" (Luke 2:15).

The writer of Psalm 66 said, "Come and see the works of God." The two events of grace that he had in mind were the Exodus and the crossing of Jordan. These were high moments in the life of Israel. Their occurrences brought forth rejoicing and the praising of

God for His goodness.

We, too, rejoice over great, high peaks that gave us the beginning of Christianity. Think of our superlative moments, those special events in which God has manifested His love and presence among us.

"There [at Bethlehem] let us rejoice in Him!" The angel told Joseph, "You shall call His name Jesus, for He will save His people from their sins" (Matthew 1:21b). He is Immanuel, "God with us." This event of His coming into the world is the high-water mark for every Christian. When we think of Jesus, we go back in our minds to the little town of Bethlehem, a place marked by prophecy (Micah 5:2), and there we rejoice in Him!

"There [at Calvary] let us rejoice in Him!" When we look at the cross, we burst into singing, "Thanks be to God, who gives us the victory through our Lord Jesus Christ" (1 Corinthians 15:57). At that rocky hill Jesus who knew no sin was made to be sin for us (2 Corinthians 5:21). In His death for the redemption of man, Jesus came into the world. The day of His crucifixion was the darkest day of history for man, because man was guilty of crucifying Him; from heaven's view, it was the brightest day because of the salvation it brought to the human race. There, at the foot of the cross, let us rejoice in Him!

"There [at the empty tomb] let us rejoice in Him!" Matthew said of the women who received an angelic

127

revelation of Christ's resurrection, "And they left the tomb quickly with fear and great joy and ran to report it to His disciples" (Matthew 28:8). Two conflicting emotions filled their hearts: fear and joy. We tremble in awe and rejoice with an exceedingly great joy at the glorious news that He is risen. The resurrection has provided the crowning proof of His deity. Two book-ends to His life confirm His deity: the virgin womb and the victorious tomb. Light, life, and immortality came into full view when He manifested His power over death. At the garden tomb, yes, there at the place of His resurrection, there where He defeated death, let us rejoice in Him!

"There [at the Ascension] let us rejoice in Him!" As we think of Jesus going through the skies to the Father's throne, our hearts are filled with praise for His earthly life and death. We can say with the writer of Hebrews, "Therefore, since we have a great high priest who has passed through the heavens, Jesus the Son of God, let us hold fast our confession" (Hebrews 4:14). As we watch intently at His going, we resolve anew that we will remember our confession. We will be faithful to our Lord as we work and await His return.

"There [at Pentecost] let us rejoice in Him!" What Isaiah saw dimly through the glass of prophecy, we are able to see through the brilliant revelation of the New Testament. The mountain of the house of the Lord has been established as the chief of the mountains. It has

been raised up above the hills, and all nations are streaming to it. People from every nation, tongue, and culture are saying, "Come, let us go up to the mountain of the Lord . . . that He may teach us concerning His ways . . ." (Isaiah 2:2, 3). We say with Paul, "To Him be the glory in the church and in Christ Jesus to all generations forever and ever" (Ephesians 3:21). Because we live as a part of His spiritual body, we look to Pentecost and declare, "There let us rejoice in Him!"

Every time these earthshaking events come to our minds, we pause and pray with thanksgiving, rejoicing in God and His Son. We have seen the glory of the Lord in His birth, crucifixion, resurrection, and ascension, as well as in His kingdom. Hallelujah! Let us spend the rest of our lives rejoicing in what God has done for us.

Of all the Old Testament worthies,
we have to say, "All these died in faith,
without receiving the promises,
but having seen them and having welcomed
them from a distance . . ." (Hebrews 11:13).

Of those living in the Christian Age, we can
say with joy, "God . . . in these last days has
spoken to us in His Son, whom He appointed
heir of all things" (Hebrews 1:1, 2a) and He
has "rescued us from the domain of darkness,

*and transferred us to the kingdom of His
beloved Son, in whom we have redemption,
the forgiveness of sins" (Colossians 1:13, 14).*

*In prayer, praise God for the specific,
superlative events that He has provided
to bring us salvation.*

41

CRYING FOR MOAB

"My heart cries out for Moab; his fugitives are as far as Zoar and Eglath-shelishiyah, for they go up the ascent of Luhith weeping; surely on the road to Horonaim they raise a cry of distress over their ruin" (Isaiah 15:5).

"When He approached Jerusalem, He saw the city and wept over it" (Luke 19:41).

"In the days of His flesh, He offered up both prayers and supplications with loud crying and tears to the One able to save Him from death . . ." (Hebrews 5:7).

One of the most unbelievable truths about Jesus, the Son of God, is that He wept. Yes, the One who made all things, while here in the flesh, wept.

Perhaps nothing moves us as much as the thought of God crying. Jesus silently wept at Lazarus' tomb as He saw the pain and hurt caused by death (John 11:35).

On His last trip into Jerusalem, He looked at this famous religious city, the city that was going to reject and crucify Him, and he cried out loud (Luke 19:41). In the Garden, as He wrestled in fervent prayer with the ordeal of His crucifixion, He engaged in much crying (Hebrews 5:7). He wept for His friends, for the lost, and for Himself. Yes, the most profound truth of all truths is that Jesus, God's Son, saw and felt the human plight and cried.

However, there is more. The oracle of judgment concerning Moab in Isaiah 15:5 makes mention of God crying: "My heart cries out for Moab." Why would anyone, especially God, weep for Moab? Moab had been an enemy of God's people all through the years. They were cruel and vicious, ruthless and violent, believing in child sacrifice and human domination. They would destroy a city without batting an eye. The people who knew the Moabites and had been afflicted by them would rejoice with enduring gladness over their destruction, but not God. He has no pleasure in the death of the wicked. He would have all to be saved and come to the knowledge of the truth (1 Timothy 2:4). He will never turn a tragedy into a comedy.

He cried out for Moab because of their sin. God's heart is touched when people turn their lives over to the devastating lifestyle of evil. As God looks at what sin has done and is doing to them, He cries out in their behalf. From the beginning, God and sin have been at war; whenever an individual or a nation surrenders to sin, God weeps.

Should we not cry out for those we know who are being swallowed up by wickedness? Do we have hearts that can be touched by the horrible predicaments of others?

God cried out for Moab because of their pain. Our God feels our pain. His heart breaks over the distress of people who do not even believe in Him. For this precise reason, Jesus wept at the tomb of Lazarus. He was not mourning for Lazarus. He knew that within minutes Lazarus would walk out of the tomb. He saw the stabbing pain in the hearts of Mary and Martha, and His seeing their tears brought sympathetic tears to His eyes.

God cried out for Moab because of their punishment. Moab was going to be wiped off the map. From Ar of Moab in the north to Kir of Moab in the south, from one end of the nation to the other, the country was going to be annihilated. The removal would come quickly as in a night. The people would be destroyed and the land would be left a barren waste.

God found no happiness in this calamity; He cried for Moab. When God closes the door of hell, He will not slam it with heavenly glee over the destruction of those who had rebelled against Him; He will close it with more sorrow than our feeble minds can possibly comprehend.

God is the Creator of all people, and He loves His creation with a deep, sacrificial love. He takes no delight in anyone's death; He finds no pleasure in anyone's punishment.

Jeremiah said, "Rachel is weeping for her children; she refuses to be comforted for her children, because they are no more" (Jeremiah 31:15b). In light of this prophecy, could we not say of God, "God is weeping for Moab; He refuses to be comforted, because Moab will be no more"? Even further, we can say of God, "He is weeping for anyone of His creation who is living without Him and who is going into the darkness of eternity without any hope. Yes, He refuses to be comforted because precious souls are passing from time to eternity and will be no more."

As God has dealt over the years
with the human race, He has been
forced to leave behind a trail of tears.

In prayer, praise God for the tears
that He has shed for all sinful people.

42

"Grace Upon Grace"

*"For of His fullness we have all received,
and grace upon grace. For the Law was given
through Moses; grace and truth were realized
through Jesus Christ" (John 1:16, 17).*

*"The next day he saw Jesus coming to him
and said, 'Behold, the Lamb of God who takes
away the sin of the world!'" (John 1:29).*

*"For by grace you have been saved through
faith; and that not of yourselves, it is the gift of
God; not as a result of works, so that no one may
boast. For we are His workmanship, created in
Christ Jesus for good works, which God prepared beforehand so that we would walk in
them" (Ephesians 2:8–10).*

John described our receiving Jesus' fullness as
our receiving "grace upon grace" (John 1:16). This
little expression has been variously translated. The

ASV and KJV have "grace for grace"; the NASB and WEB have "grace upon grace"; the NIV has "receiving one blessing after another"; and Young's translation has "grace over against grace."[1]

Regardless of the way this phrase is translated, it obviously is expressing the bountiful nature of His grace, the fullness and completeness of His grace, as one act of His grace piled upon another. His grace is multifaceted and multi-supplying; it not only meets our spiritual needs but it imparts to us God's gracious spirit.

Look at the different aspects of it.

It is salvational grace. Paul said, "For by grace you have been saved" (Ephesians 2:8a). Jesus' earthly appearance is the appearance of God's grace in its fullest form (Titus 2:11, 12). Jesus came to be the epitome of God's grace to us by coming to save us from our sins.

It is sustaining grace. We stand in it. We have not only been saved by grace, but we are kept saved by it. Paul said, "Through whom also we have obtained our introduction by faith into this grace in which we stand" (Romans 5:2a). When one stands in His grace, he is daily cleansed and redeemed by it. The Christian lives his life inside the marvelous covering of God's grace.

---

[1]Robert Young, *Young's Literal Translation of the Holy Bible* (Grand Rapids, Mich.: Baker Book House, 1956).

He is clothed with it. He puts Christ on in his baptism (Galatians 3:27), and he wears Christ from then on as his covering of grace. Paul said that the Christian is found in Him, not having a righteousness of his own derived from the Law, but a righteousness which is through faith in Christ, the righteousness which comes from God on the basis of faith (Philippians 3:9).

It is compassionate grace. Its workings in our lives provide the spiritual energy and sympathetic spirit by which we can be gracious to others. Paul even refers to our giving as grace (2 Corinthians 8:7). We not only stand in it, but we also serve through it.

Stephen died praying that the Lord would not lay this sin, the sin of his stoning, to the charge of those who were killing him (Acts 7:59, 60). Where did Stephen get such a beautiful spirit? The grace that filled his heart prompted him to pray this prayer of forgiveness for his murderers.

Paul said, "Let the word of Christ richly dwell within you, with all wisdom teaching and admonishing one another with psalms and hymns and spiritual songs, singing with thankfulness in your hearts to God" (Colossians 3:16). The word for "thankfulness" was translated "grace" by the ASV.

Here then is the circle of God's compassion: It goes from grace to grace. We are saved by grace, we stand in it, we serve through it, we manifest a generous, forgiving spirit toward others because it indwells us, and we naturally sing out of the joy that it brings! As the fullness of Jesus enters our lives, we have received it in the form of "grace upon grace." We could change the great hymn a little bit and actually sing, "Amazing 'grace upon grace,' that saved a wretch like me!"

We are birthed into His kingdom by His grace, we live in Christ by His grace, and at death we will enter the everlasting kingdom by His grace. We have received from Jesus acts of grace piled on top of each other.

In prayer, praise God for the multitudinous deeds of grace that He gives us.

Now and Forevermore—
A Life of Praise

> "'I will get up and go to my father, and will say to him, "Father, I have sinned against heaven, and in your sight; I am no longer worthy to be called your son; make me as one of your hired men."' So he got up and came to his father. But while he was still a long way off, his father saw him and felt compassion for him, and ran and embraced him and kissed him. And the son said to him, 'Father, I have sinned against heaven and in your sight; I am no longer worthy to be called your son.' But the father said to his slaves, 'Quickly bring out the best robe and put it on him, and put a ring on his hand and sandals on his feet; and bring the fattened calf, kill it, and let us eat and celebrate; for this son of mine was dead and has come to life again; he was lost and has been found.' . . ." (Luke 15:18–24).

In one circumstance or another, each of us has been like the prodigal in our Lord's parable. We have turned our backs on the way of sin, and we have gone back in hope and anticipation toward our Father's house. Perhaps it was when we became Christians through faith in Christ (John 8:24), repentance (Acts 17:30, 31), confession of Jesus (Romans 10:10), and baptism into Christ (Romans 6:3, 4). It may have been when we wandered away from God after we became Christians; and, after a time in the far country, we returned to Him to seek His forgiveness. Whatever the nature of our coming to Him, we have seen God run to us with His loving grace. In holy eagerness God pursued us as the One who loves us with a love that is stronger than life. He was persistent and unrelenting, refusing to give up on us even when we had given up on ourselves.

The fact that we have seen God run to us should be sufficient motivation (although we have countless other reasons) to spend the rest of our earthly lives praising Him for His great salvation.

Charles B. Hodge, Jr., with pathos and vividness, has put it like this:

> There was a son like the prodigal who disgraced his father's name and broke his mother's heart. The father became gray headed in disgrace. The mother died prematurely in grief. The son was sent to the Huntsville, Texas penitentiary. But this jail house became this young man's "hog pen." He "came to himself." He changed, he reformed. The guards

noticed it and reported it to the warden. The warden reported it to the governor and to the Board of Pardons. After several years' residency in that prison, the son was pardoned. The mustering out pay was given the young man, and he bought a train ticket to the far side of Texas. He also bought himself another suit of clothes. He went to the telegraph station and sent a wire to his dad. The telegram read, "Dad, I killed Mother. I have broken your heart and disgraced your name. I am not worthy to be called your son. But I've changed. And the governor has pardoned me. And I want to come home. I bought a train ticket that will carry me through my old home town. And, Dad, if you'll forgive me and take me back, please tie a white flag in the old apple tree down by the railroad track. Father, if you cannot, then I'll just pass through and never bother you again."

You can see the anticipation and sweat growing as the son boards the train, and you can hear the clickety-clackety, clickety-clackety clicks of the rails as the train moves along. You can hear the conductor as he sings out the stations along the way. Finally, as this reaches climactic proportion, the conductor rings out the name of the young man's home town. The son places his hand over his eyes and closes his eyes tightly—he is afraid to look. But out of necessity the hands are removed and the eyes are opened. And he sees the apple tree. There was not that one flag in that apple tree. There were a thousand! Beloved, the father was afraid something might happen to a few. And he wanted his son to know he had been forgiven,

he was wanted back! What a wonderful day when the
prodigal came home.[1]

This drama of a prodigal returning to his father's
heart is not just a human interest story from the news-
paper; it is your story and mine. God ran to meet us and
made us His sons and daughters. He put the robe of
grace upon our shoulders, the ring of sonship on our
fingers, and the sandals of honor and purpose on our
feet.

Yes, God covered the antediluvian world with the
water of judgment, but He did not run to do it. He
burned Sodom and Gomorrah to ashes, but He did not
run to do it. You will see Him running for only one
purpose. He runs to make us His children by cleansing
and forgiving us.

If you are His child, you have seen Him run. He ran
to meet you, He put His arms around you, He cleansed
you of all your sins, and He made you His son or
daughter.

With His great and generous love, He has won us
over. We have given our hearts to Him. Through Jesus,
our Savior, we are now safe with our Father! Constrained by His lovingkindness, we will follow His
Word and praise Him! We will join with the great host
that has gone before in the grandest anthems that

---

[1]Charles B. Hodge, Jr., *Will God Run?* (Searcy, Ark.: Resource
Publications, 2002), 20–21.

human lips can phrase and sing—the choruses of praise!

"Worthy are You, our Lord and our God,
to receive glory and honor and power;
for You created all things, and
because of Your will they existed,
and were created" (Revelation 4:11).

"Worthy is the Lamb that was slain
to receive power and riches and wisdom
and might and honor and glory
and blessing" (Revelation 5:12).

"After these things I looked, and behold,
a great multitude which no one could count,
from every nation and all tribes and peoples
and tongues, standing before the throne and
before the Lamb, clothed in white robes, and
palm branches were in their hands; and they
cry out with a loud voice, saying, 'Salvation to
our God who sits on the throne, and to the
Lamb.' And all the angels were standing
around the throne and around the elders and
the four living creatures; and they fell on their
faces before the throne and worshiped God,
saying, "Amen, blessing and glory and
wisdom and thanksgiving and honor

and power and might, be to our God forever
and ever. Amen" (Revelation 7:9–12).

"I saw no temple in it, for the Lord God
the Almighty and the Lamb are its temple.
And the city has no need of the sun or
of the moon to shine on it, for the glory
of God has illumined it, and its lamp
is the Lamb" (Revelation 21:22, 23).

For the rest of our lives, let us love and adore Him! To our God and His Son be the glory in time and eternity!

TRUTH FOR TODAY
WORLD MISSION SCHOOL

The author of this book is the director of
Truth for Today World Mission School,
located in Searcy, Arkansas.

This school provides a worldwide
printed training school in the Scriptures.

You are invited to learn more
about the school by visiting its website:
www.biblecourses.com.